P9-CPW-636

The Teaching for Social Justice Series

William Ayers—Series Editor
Therese Quinn—Associate Series Editor

Advance Praise for *Spectacular Things Happen Along the Way*

"This fifth-grade class illustrates some important lessons about America: The neglect of the inner-city poor, the virtues of creative public service, of teaching to educate—not just to pass a test—and of perseverance."
                    —**Robert Siegel,** *All Things Considered,* National Public Radio

"Stories about these problems . . . had turned Carr into a national symbol of the squalid inequalities in public education. And Schultz's pupils had come to represent the frustrations and untapped determination of children who attend dilapidated schools."
                                                          —**Chicago Tribune**

"Carr Community Academy is a crumbling elementary school in Chicago next to one of the largest and most perilous public housing projects—Cabrini Green. It also is the location of one of the more spectacular fifth-grade classes in the country."
                    —**Ralph Nader,** consumer advocate, author,
                    and founder, Public Citizen research group

"When city kids are thought to be nothing more than a tangle of pathologies and deficits who must somehow be 'saved' by crusading, missionary teachers, the result is always some form of colonization. In this extraordinary book, Brian Schultz, a courageous teacher writing here with clarity and passion, performs a radical reversal and provides an alternative."
                    —**William Ayers,** Distinguished Professor of Education,
                    University of Illinois at Chicago, and author of *To Teach*

"In this era of high-stakes testing and prescriptive curriculum, it is essential that we have books like this one to act as a counterweight to many of the grim realities new teachers are facing."
                    —**Celia Oyler,** Teachers College, Columbia University

"Creating curriculum together, Brian Schultz and his Room 405 warrior students studied through struggling for a new school. A torrid tale of hope for us all."
                    —**William F. Pinar,** Canada Research Chair,
                    University of British Columbia

"Through their compelling school improvement efforts, Schultz and his fifth graders clearly counter the colonizing policy that says only the privileged can be educated through freedom to pursue personal interests and collective commitments."
                    —**William H. Schubert,** University Scholar,
                    University of Illinois at Chicago

Spectacular Things Happen Along the Way

LESSONS FROM AN URBAN CLASSROOM

Brian D. Schultz

foreword by
CARL A. GRANT

Teachers College
Columbia University
New York and London

Cover photo copyright © 2008 Phyllis Burstein

Published by Teachers College Press, 1234 Amsterdam Avenue, New York, NY 10027

Library of Congress Cataloging-in-Publication Data

Schultz, Brian D.
  Spectacular things happen along the way : lessons from an urban classroom / Brian D. Schultz ; foreword by Carl A. Grant.
      p. cm. — (The teaching for social justice series)
  Includes bibliographical reference and index.
  ISBN 978-0-8077-4857-2 (pbk. : alk. paper) — ISBN 978-0-8077-4858-9 (hardcover : alk. paper)
  1. Community and school—United States. 2. Home and school—United States.
3. School improvement programs—United States. I. Title.
  LC215.S388 2008
  370.9173'2—dc22

                                                                                    2007048322

ISBN 978-0-8077-4857-2 (paper)
ISBN 978-0-8077-4858-9 (cloth)

Printed on acid-free paper
Manufactured in the United States of America

15   14   13   12   11   8   7   6   5   4

To the former students of Room 405 at Carr Community Academy, without whose creativity, imagination, and fortitude these stories would not have been possible.

And, to Jenn and Addison, with love

I LEARN FROM CHILDREN

—Caroline Pratt

Contents

Foreword

When I read Brian Schultz's *Spectacular Things Happen Along the Way: Lessons from an Urban Classroom,* I approached it as both a professional and personal assignment. Brian and I are colleagues with similar concerns about how to educate all students and how to prepare teachers for urban schools. I am always on alert for ideas about how to work successfully with urban students.

I have, however, become a very cautious reader and scholar, because I am often disappointed with what I read about educating students who live in urban areas. Since the 1960s, there has been a regular stream of books about teaching urban, low-income students of color. Most of these stories are desperately wanting. Many have weak, formulaic storylines involving a White teacher–savior and street-smart but academically inept Black and Brown students. Yet, with the publication of his book, Brian Schultz challenges this, embodying an idea which I sincerely believe: A teacher's skin color does not have a negative effect on the ability to be successful teaching students of a different color. *Spectacular Things Happen Along the Way* renewed my belief that it is possible to write *authentic* narratives about urban schools.

In Brian's book, you meet a teacher who struggles with the circumstances of school life and who continually challenges himself by reflecting upon how to improve. In the students he writes about, you see a move from uncertainty of self and ability to a development of agency and academic confidence. You learn that the students in Room 405 are capable of rigorous learning. You are also reminded that education is not neutral, but very political: Race and socioeconomic status are significant factors that determine how and which children are sorted out and denied equality and social justice.

I plan to make Brian's book required reading for my teacher education students because it answers two prevailing questions in the mind of the mostly White students entering teacher education programs: "Can I successfully teach students of color?" and "Will students of color reject the 'acting White mantra' and do what it takes to be successful in school?" These are significant questions for all teachers and they are questions that have challenged outstanding thinkers and writers, including Carter G. Woodson, James Baldwin, and Malcolm X.

In his 1933 book, *The Mis-Education of the Negro*, Carter G. Woodson questioned teachers' capacity, paying particular attention to the dispositions of White teachers teaching Negro children:

> To be frank we must concede that there is no particular body of facts that Negro teachers can impart to children of their own race that may not be just as easily presented by persons of another race if they have the same attitude as Negro teachers; but in most cases tradition, race, hate, segregation, and terrorism make such a thing impossible. (p. 28)

Similarly, when James Baldwin spoke to teachers in 1963, he claimed, "[We] are living through a very dangerous time. . . . Teaching black children is revolutionary." In concluding, Baldwin declared, "It is your responsibility to change society if you think of yourself as an educated person." However, he cautioned, " . . . [Y]ou will meet the most fantastic, the most brutal, and the most determined resistance" since "what societies really, ideally want is a citizenry which will simply obey the rules of society."

The students of Room 405 demonstrate a no-nonsense understanding of the purpose of education, and their actions symbolize the words of Malcolm X. In a 1964 speech he stated: "Education is our passport to the future, for tomorrow belongs to the people who prepare for it today" (quoted in Riley, 1993, p. 320). The intense commitment to the curriculum shows Room 405's understanding that the passport was not the new school, but rather the education received in pursuit. The students learned the necessary foundations to achieve personal and professional agency and a flourishing life, and prepared to become civic servants and leaders.

When I finished Brian's book, I was troubled because a fantastic teacher has left a school system that, like most urban school systems, desperately needs outstanding teachers. Nonetheless I am also encouraged that Brian has, in moving on, written this account and dedicated himself to teaching those interested in learning how to be successful teachers in urban spaces, thus addressing another area of great concern and need.

Carl A. Grant

Preface and Acknowledgments

This book is a narrative account of one teacher's journey. It is about a teacher being reflective about his classroom practice, while simultaneously it is about kids, particularly ones from an urban housing project, being political based on what is most important to them. The book is organized as a reconstruction of my thought processes and my interpretation of a year-long classroom experience with fifth graders from Chicago's Cabrini Green neighborhood. When the elementary students in Room 405 were challenged to name problems in their school and community, they unanimously focused on replacing their dilapidated school building. Rather than this being a simple activity, addressing this complicated issue became our curriculum for the remainder of the school year. The narrative storytelling central to the book portrays the fifth graders' attempts at solving this complex problem through a curriculum that we developed together.

Because of the nature of the classroom curriculum portrayed here, there are undoubtedly numerous people who need to be sincerely thanked for standing by and supporting me to make the classroom and its portrayal a reality. First and foremost, the students in Room 405—the inspiration for the stories here—deserve my heartfelt thanks. I learned so much from each young person in our classroom. They taught me and continue to teach me more than I could ever have hoped to teach them. In my text, each student's name has been changed, and some students' personalities, characteristics, or actions have even been combined or altered to protect their identities and keep personal matters confidential. However, the essence of their story—fortitude and charisma—is intact, and the narrative accounts are my honest interpretation of the classroom experience. I have attempted to make students' voices prominent in the vignettes through direct quotations from classroom talk or classroom artifacts. To preserve the authenticity of the children's voices, passages in the book written by students are verbatim and uncorrected. Further, I know that if one of my students were to tell any of these stories, they might be very different from my account.

In addition to the students of Room 405, it is necessary to recognize the administration, teachers, and staff at Chicago Public School's William D. Carr Community Academy (also a pseudonym). Their dedication to teaching and children is tremendous—an example for others to follow. I learned so much from all of them.

This book began as my doctoral dissertation at the University of Illinois at Chicago. I am extremely thankful to my dissertation chair, teacher, and friend, William H. Schubert. Bill's dedication and accessibility have truly helped me think through the big curriculum questions and what it means to be a teacher. By pushing me to ponder and wonder about questions of worth, Bill helped me to rethink what education, schooling, learning, and life are all about. Others on my dissertation committee also had a profound effect on me and the evolution of this book. Thanks to Bill Ayers, Greg Michie, Dave Stovall, and Ward Weldon for the excellent insight, challenges, wisdom, and knowledge they shared with me.

Along the way, many fellow graduate students, colleagues, and friends offered insight and encouragement, helping to shape my thinking about this project. I owe a debt of gratitude to all those who were moved, like me, by the fifth graders of Room 405. Those of you who got involved, many without any sort of compensation or formal recognition, need to be commended: David Ablao, Jill Adams, James Beane, Brian Billings, Todd Bittorf, Adrienne Boutwell, Marion Brady, Judy Brakes, Jessica Chethik, Niki Christodoulou, Margarita Daronk, Willie Delgado, Miguel del Valle, Michael Fischer, Monica Garcia, Joseph Gartner, Sarah Goley, Peter Hilton, Cheryl James, Terry Jones, Young Joo Kim, Tom Kopp, Kristi Madda, Ralph Nader, Mitchell Norinksy, Isabel Nuñez, Cassandra McKay, Celia Oyler, Carl Owens, Karen Percak, Therese Quinn, Ann Lynn Lopez Schubert, Debbie Sheriff, Gini Sorrentinni, Brad Stein, Steve Tozer, Eric Zorn, Room 405 parents, the Center for Civic Education, the Collaboratory writing mentors, the Constitutional Rights Foundation Chicago, and all the folks who recognized and wrote on the students' behalf (including those accidentally overlooked) and who certainly did make a difference in the lives of these young people. I am especially indebted to Pamela Konkol and Jason Lukasik for their assistance and dedication throughout the project and the writing process. Their perspective and feedback, in addition to their excellent eyes and critical commentary, have provided great intellectual companionship. Also, thanks to Phyllis Burstein, for all her involvement during the school year and for the expertise editing the images taken by Room 405 students throughout the book.

Thanks to the wonderful people at Teachers College Press, who offered tremendous feedback and guidance on my work throughout the publishing process: Judy Berman, Tamar Elster, Susan Liddicoat, Golnar Nikpour, Carole Saltz, Leyli Shayegan, Aureliano Vazquez, and Leah Wonski.

My parents' value of education and, more importantly, lifelong learning has been my muse. Whether listening to my chatter of ideas or critiquing my writing, my parents have always been there for me. Appreciation also to Amy, whose encouragement and her own pursuits are motivating and invigorating. Hugs to Jenn and Addison, Mom and David, Dad and Jane, Amy and Chris, the Grands, Grandma Lenore, Melani, Matthew, Renee, and Lily. Also thanks to Ken Addison, Dan Baxt, Diane Ehrlich, Debra Freedman, Walter Gershon, Maureen Gillette, Carl Grant, Mike Gross, Ross Holzman, Scott Henry, Sherick Hughes, Nicole Holland, Jeff Hulett, Sheri Leafgren, Elaine Koffman, Art Kopittke, Craig Kridel, Eleni Makris, Erica Meiners, Jim McBride, Sharon McNeely, Brian Murphy, Michael O'Malley, NEIU colleagues, Patrick Reichard, Patrick Roberts, Josh Simon, Casey Stuelpe, Adam Schlesinger, Durene Wheeler, Ann Whitaker, Stan Wilson, and Mo Zahrawi.

Throughout the entire process of writing this book, my wife Jennifer has been steadfast and amazing. I cannot express in words how thankful I am for her patience, guidance, and wonderful ability to listen to my seemingly endless talk. She vicariously lived many of the experiences told throughout the book (most willingly). Beyond encouragement, her first reads, insight, endless editing, thoughtful questioning, willingness to hear my ideas, and ability to stand by me even when she was understandably "tired of it" cannot be matched. I look forward to continuing to share our lives together with Addison.

Spectacular Things
Happen Along the Way

Embracing Students' Interests for Schoolwork

WHAT'S WORTH KNOWING?

The noise level amplified in Room 405. The fifth-grade students shouted out ideas as I tried to keep up with their growing list. The intensity was beyond measurement as students called out problems affecting them: "teenage pregnancy," "litter in the park," even "stopping Michael Jackson!" A lot of the problems had to do with their school, Carr Community Academy: "foggy windows pocked with bullet holes," "no lunchroom, gym, or auditorium," "clogged toilets," and "broken heaters in the classroom." Before long, the fifth graders identified 89 different problems affecting them and their community, a challenge posed just an hour earlier.

As the list grew and I hurriedly marked up the chalkboard with their ideas, some students began arguing with one another that a problem they proposed had already been mentioned. Insightfully, Dyneisha cut through the ensuing debate and stated, "Most of the problems on that list have to do with our school building bein' messed up. Our school is a dump! That's

the problem." With this profound analysis there was a sense of affirmation in the room, and the students unanimously agreed the most pressing issue was the poor condition and inadequacy of their school building. As I looked out at the students gathered together on that cold December morning, I was confronted by just how true that realization was. Most were wearing hats, gloves, and coats in the classroom, exemplifying the real

problem they were living. They were very perceptive in citing the numerous problems with the school. These students knew them well; they had lived this injustice their entire school-aged lives.

In short order, the fifth graders listed major problems in need of fixing. In asking the question, I had anticipated the students might decide on simpler tasks like wanting fruit punch at lunch or trying to get recess every day. Instead they went for a more challenging issue, one that had existed in the community for years: A new school had been promised but was never built. I wondered to myself whether these students were really willing to tackle this problem head-on. Before I could even ask, they were already suggesting ways they might remedy problems with the school structure and constructing plans to get a new school built. Given the opportunity and challenge to prioritize a problem in their community, the children were not only willing to itemize the issues but were already strategizing ways to make change. And so this emergent curriculum began.

Project Citizen

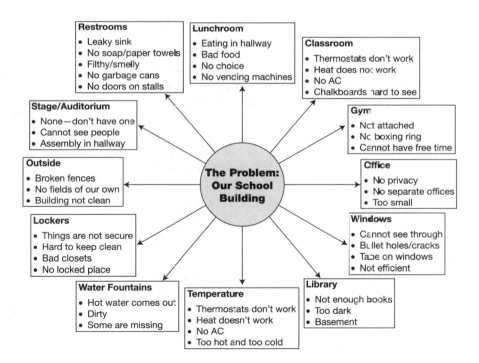

Framing the Situation: The Context of Cabrini Green

While teaching and learning with my students, who reside in Chicago public housing, I continually affirmed my notion that the role of the teacher is to provide opportunity and space to students. The teacher ultimately must embrace intelligence, allowing students to leverage what they know and what they can successfully accomplish. As the students develop this essential opportunity, their imagination, interest, and creativity allow them to create a love for their learning that may endure the travesties and injustices they face both in and out of the classroom.

Just up the street from Chicago's downtown "Loop" business district, according to most media accounts, is one of the most notorious and infamous housing projects in the United States. The reputation of Cabrini Green often precedes it—best known for drugs and gangs, and synonymous with the failing social programs and initiatives meant to help low-income people.

As with most of the public housing in Chicago, the Cabrini Green Homes are in the midst of massive redevelopment and gentrification. Located immediately north of the Chicago River on what was once declared slum land, the high-rise apartment tenements and their accompanying row houses were originally built over a 20-year period from the early 1940s through the 1960s. Named to honor America's first saint, the Cabrini Green development was originally conceived as temporary housing. Veterans returning from World War II were Cabrini's first inhabitants, and initially the area was populated by a racially and ethnically diverse group of residents.

Soon after completion of the housing project, the city of Chicago faced a significant economic hardship. The routine upkeep and critical maintenance of the Cabrini Green Homes ceased almost as soon as the last brick was laid. The high-density buildings quickly deteriorated. In efforts to save additional funds, the city stopped most police patrols, and gang activity took over the 70-acre area that butted up against some of Chicago's most affluent neighborhoods. City services, such as trash pickup and public transportation, refused to stop in the area citing safety concerns. Rat and roach infestations plagued the area. Underground economies took over, while the negligence gained national attention. Burned-out facades and boarded-up windows from multiple fires as well as decaying apartment buildings were an eyesore, and their mismanagement became symbolic of urban blight and everything wrong with public housing. The residents who were able to get out of the area did, but the people with the least resources who called Cabrini Green home found this impossible. Cabrini Green became this group's permanent residence as its original temporary status was superseded. The approximate 18,000 units, originally integrated with notable diversity, became almost exclusively occupied by African Americans (Peterson, 1997).

Cabrini Green differs from many other housing projects. Instead of being relegated to an industrial corridor or an undesirable area, Cabrini was built in what currently is the popular Old Town neighborhood, sits adjacent to the prestigious Lincoln Park, and lies in shadows of the exclusive skyscrapers of the Magnificent Mile and Gold Coast. Because of this proximity to high-priced real estate and its desirable locale, the property has become extremely valuable. In recent years, the city and the Chicago Housing Authority (CHA) have developed a public relations and Madison-Avenue-style advertising campaign to support the plan to redevelop the area. Allegedly making it available for mixed-income families, the CHA's "Plan for Transformation" has created a hotbed of controversy. Hyped as an example for other urban areas to emulate, the reality of the plan involves displacing and uprooting the African American residents. The CHA and city let the properties deteriorate so much that the Authority itself declared the apartments unlivable, clearing the way to receive federal permission to demolish and redesign the community.

Almost every account I have read or seen about Chicago's poverty-stricken Cabrini Green describes the area as a haven for drugs and murder, gang-banging, misery, and mayhem. Even in an article praising my students' work, the author reported, "Cabrini Green Homes has all the stuff of which failure is made, and it often delivers door-to-door" (Brady, 2004, p. A19). Much of this portrayal may be accurate, but the story of the residents, especially the children, is rarely told. Within this community there are young kids with many needs. They require the same or better instruction, dedication, and nurturing as any other student in any other area. In addition, the students are capable citizens and good thinkers with untapped creativity who need the opportunity to demonstrate and practice their intelligences. My student Tavon stated it best: "Even though our neighborhood has problems, we are proud of our neighborhood. This is why we are fighting for a better school. We think everyone should have a good home and a good school."

Because of the challenging conditions associated with Cabrini Green, coupled with societal issues and constraints, the perennial question of *what is worth knowing* is constantly raised by my students. An understanding of how students from this neighborhood learn is imperative, as they continually adapt in a practical sense. Prior to our time together, they told me, there was little nurturing of the strengths or abilities learned outside of school, but rather a devaluing of their adaptive and street intelligences. Many could not endure, as one student put it, "life in the projects without bein' street-smart or learnin' how to survive . . . because there are a lot of people who are gonna test you." At the same time, they are seldom recognized in school for their achievements outside the classroom. If education was measured by the students' successes in their neighborhood via their own lived experiences, many would outperform their more affluent peers, not to mention their teachers. As I pondered this situation, I wondered how we could best draw on the students' adaptability and street savvy in school. Could an authentic and integrated curriculum focusing on students' interests and concerns emerge and be successful in the "traditional" classroom?

Documenting and Reaching Out

None of us knew where attempting to solve the problems of the school building would take us, but with the momentum from our initial class discussion and consensus about focusing on the school building, the students and I went forward.

With the students' interest in the school's condition as the starting point, the classroom evolved into one in which authority was shared between students and teacher; students decided how and what they would do to enact their daily curriculum and ultimately became agents of social change based on what mattered most to them. The students' analyses and descriptions would set the stage for ways the class could try to resolve the issue. This investigation would lead students to examine alternative solutions for solving the predicament in which they found themselves and subsequently let the students focus on a specific idea, namely, the need to secure a new school building for the community and force the decision makers to fulfill their erstwhile promise. Strategizing and enacting ways of solving the problem would become the curriculum.

Although there was a clear problem to solve, and we knew there was the need for some sort of plan to accomplish our goals, none of us really knew where to begin. The students' verve drove us to begin documenting problems in the school with photographs and writing expository text about its shortcomings. The students produced astonishing, sophisticated compositions. When asked how they were able to construct such work in a rough draft, Demetrius responded, "This stuff is really important, and I need to get the word out if I want something done." These rough drafts became the starting point, and getting the word out is exactly what they did. Quickly realizing the drafts needed to be transformed into persuasive statements, the students and I compiled their individual work to create a powerful letter they sent to the school board, city officials, newspaper reporters, and concerned citizens. In the letter, the students provocatively documented the big problems about their school that were not fixable and wrote, "We would like to invite you to see our school for yourself. We do not think you would let your kids come to a school that is falling apart."

Responses came pouring in immediately. Phone inquiries, letters, e-mails, and visits from legislators, as well as newspaper and TV reporters, kept the students' project flowing with questions, suggestions, and encouragement. In going beyond the classroom walls, the students quickly became engaged in real-life curricula. As the class made its concerns known, many people offered insight, assistance, donations, and publicity. Taking into account advice from these outsiders, the students put together a comprehensive action plan they believed would help get their perfect solution— a whole new school.

The students' action plan became the epicenter of the entire curriculum for the remainder of the school year. Every subject lost its compartmentalization, becoming integrated and integral in solving the problem. Reading, writing, arithmetic, and social studies were all blended together. Rather than using basal textbooks, the students researched pertinent information about how to solve their problem. Their search took them to texts beyond their reading level and aptitude, but they were willing to put forth the effort because it had value to their situation. While reading from Jonathan Kozol's (1992) *Savage Inequalities*, one boy appropriately remarked, "I think this book was written 'bout us. The author must of come to Carr school." And his statement was not far from the truth, as Chester documented in his expository writing,

> The restrooms are filthy and dirty. It is really smelly in the bathrooms
> because the toilets don't flush. As an example of how bad they are,
> sinks move . . . water leaks everywhere. And we do not even have
> soap or paper towels. Kids don't use the bathrooms no more since
> they are so gross!

Reading flowed into current events as students reacted to newspaper articles written about them. In addition, they read about techniques for par-

ticipation, which showed them how to do things like survey and petition. The students learned how to prepare documentation, including questionnaire results, photos, and written assessments, as they incorporated data analysis and mathematics into their student-driven curriculum to gain support. After taking this documentation to the public, one student asserted, "No one who saw our folders could disagree with what we were saying about the school's problems." To get more folks involved and aware, students developed a Web site to organize all the materials and artifacts they had accumulated. This was no small task as they had pictures and writing from visits of politicians and researchers, hundreds of letters written on their behalf, journal entries, petitions, charts, graphs, surveys, and analyses.

Room 405 became a headquarters to "make important decisions about who we should bring in to help," according to one student's journal entry. It was a think tank for investigating ways "we can better get others involved," documented another. Transforming the classroom into a campaign office, students assumed roles of leadership in their quest, and as Jaris commented in his journal, "Being an interviewer . . . makes me feel like a business manager. It makes me feel real important and other kids look up to me. This has never happened to me in school before." The students were so involved in the development of their curriculum they came early, left late, and even showed up on days off to get the job done.

Looking Back

Frustrated by a hidden curriculum based on social class, I was looking for a compromise that would keep my students motivated and engaged in their learning while teaching them the necessary skills base to progress in school. Challenging the notion of teaching students differently according to their socioeconomic class, I sought the equity in teaching and learning that I so strongly felt the students deserved. My initial wondering led me to revisit essential questions with students regarding what knowledge is most worthwhile:

- Ultimately, what would happen if Room 405 at Carr Community Academy in Cabrini Green took on an experiment of our own?
- What if the teacher and students decided in an educational setting to problem-pose, challenge, and deliberate like their counterparts in affluent schools?
- Could the curriculum be driven by student interest to meet situational needs?
- Would others listen to our voices and concerns?
- What would be the consequences of our actions?
- Would we be able to go beyond following the rules and assert creative ideals?
- Could we challenge the status quo to make the curriculum of, by, and for us?
- Or, as one of the girls in the class asked, "Who's gonna listen to a bunch of Black kids from Cabrini Green?"

There was only one way to find out.

Using these questions as a framework for a democratic curriculum, and inspired by a Project Citizen workshop that promoted a curricular framework encouraging teachers and students to engage in citizen action and public policy change, I created a space for the students to embark on an experience in learning how the government works and ways in which they might become actively involved in bringing about social change. As I look back, I remember a conversation with several students in which Dyneisha summarized our work in the classroom as a "way to learn how the government works and ways to work the government." By embracing a meaningful problem, the curriculum became a catalyst for authentic, integrated learning to occur.

Through the project, the students were given the opportunity and responsibility to be active participants in the development and design of their own learning. The comments of Crown, a chronic truant prior to participating in this classroom, resonate strongly: "I did not feel school was a place for me. I didn't think it would help me in my life, but this project made me like coming to school. . . . It did not feel like the boring school I was used to." His turnaround and newfound dedication to schoolwork and attendance demonstrated the power of a democratic classroom, where students were critical members encouraged to embrace their own ideas of what is worthwhile.

As their teacher, I learned that content can come from the students rather than be driven into them by artificial objectives. Just as students in the more affluent schools are encouraged and rewarded for insight and creativity, these urban, African American students could make their voices heard through purposeful action and determination.

There were certainly risks involved in trying to solve authentic curriculum problems and create democratic ideals in a classroom. Students were no longer protected by contrived lesson plans and people cast doubt as to whether students, especially inner-city African Americans, were capable of taking on a real problem. Even the school's extremely supportive principal initially had reservations about lessons students might learn from the project. In a National Public Radio interview he said, "If they don't see things happening, I am afraid that they are going to say, voice all you want, but your voice is a small voice and doesn't matter" (Glass, 2004). Today, though, everyone, including the principal, would argue that the lessons taken away from the project were immeasurable. Terrance succinctly summed up this idea in a journal entry:

> We would love to get our perfect solution of getting a new school built, but we have figured out that great things can happen when you fight for what is right. . . . Even though we are not getting a new school we have done great things . . . like it said in one of the letters supporting us, "Spectacular things happen along the way!"

As I write this account several years later, I remain in contact with many former students. The curriculum we developed together has had a lasting impact on all of us. Opportunities to tell our story continue to emerge, and I often share my writing with the former students from Room 405. Going over some text with Crown, I asked, "Who am I as a White, middle-class teacher to write about you guys?" He looked me directly in the eye and said, "To me you ain't speaking outta turn because you not talkin' bad or nothin' about Black people . . . you taking they side and feelin' what they feelin'." I only hope that I can, perhaps, live up to his words.

"INVERTING" THE CURRICULUM

The opening vignette provides a glimpse into a classroom where the students, along with their teacher, developed a curriculum together. But what does it mean to create curriculum together, and how did this experience evolve? The classroom was structured in such a way that the curriculum revolved around the interests and needs of the students and emerged out of students' efforts to solve an important problem. But this classroom experience did not happen by chance. Certain ideas, situations, and experiences came together to provide this opportunity for all of us.

The time I spent reading material on social justice–oriented teaching in my doctoral studies, while I was a classroom teacher, reinforced my belief that the most desirable curriculum for children is one that comes from them. This dual identity as both a teacher and a student opened a new window of opportunity into my classroom and role as an educator. However, allowing students to decide what they want to study and how they want to approach their learning is not the norm in most schools. I wondered what such a curriculum would look like. How would and could a curriculum created by students and their teacher be incorporated into a traditional school? Was this concept even a possibility in the current climate of high-stakes testing and accountability?

In schools today, it seems that everything revolves around standards, accountability, and measurement. Rather than focusing on students' abilities to learn through problem solving, student achievement is often assessed by performance on high-stakes tests supposedly aligned with state standards. These standards, developed by state boards of education, create an awkwardness students and teachers struggle with daily. The awkwardness stems from the fact that school districts, school principals, and teachers use these objectives as front-loaded points for lesson plans or checklists. Whereas planning curriculum in schools should have clear-cut goals, outlining specific expectations, including standards, absent from the interactions of particular classrooms is artificial. Standards do not take particular schools into account and, thus, are often misinterpreted and misused in curriculum development. This incorrect use of standards makes attaining them unrealistic for classrooms with varying abilities and also forces learning into an impractical act. While standards prescribed by governing bodies may serve as guides and represent expectations, they do not reflect a comprehensive understanding of individualized needs and certainly do not account for what happens in classrooms as children problem-solve and interact with their learning.

Like most teachers, I wanted my students to meet or exceed these standards. But what value did the standard have in the absence of purposeful action? Administrators, teachers, and publishing companies all over the country seem to believe that by stating that the particular objective is being covered it is automatically understood, realized, and applied by students. Unfortunately, this approach is all too common, and in many schools it is even required.

Interpreting standards quite differently from others around me, I believed authentic learning—solving an actual problem—could actually meet standards by organically emerging out of the classroom curriculum. This approach would meet the objectives not for their own sake, but because the behaviors and outcomes outlined in the standards were necessary components in solving the problem. If the classroom curriculum was inverted so that students' pursuits led them to the outcome of meeting standards, the class members' ideas could be at the forefront, rather than what someone else expected them to know or understand at a particular time. Guided by a facilitating teacher, this experiential approach encourages each student's growth and nurtures individual development.

In our classroom, I spent very little time tailoring lessons or activities to standards; rather, we developed criteria based on what we felt was most important. When this occurred, prescribed standards such as "reading with fluency" or "reading for understanding" were met. Students wanted the opportunity to make sense of topics important to them. This was clearly evident, for example, when the students investigated how the state spent its budget, read budgetary guidelines, and analyzed other documents they had researched on the Internet. Because their interest was the starting point, the reading-related standards did not need to be front-loaded. Instead of coming from the outside, these standards came from within the students as a means to get a job done. The students in my classroom fluidly searched for relevant information. In order to understand how something worked, subject matters were rarely separated unnaturally into disciplines; instead the students worked together to make learning pertinent. Through interaction with the students, I discovered that adhering to imposed standards should not be driven by the standards themselves. Rather, the process should be driven by the priority concerns of the students. In this way meaningful interfacing with the environment helped the students to develop purposeful curricula revolving around themselves and their community, where standards were the outcomes necessary to reaching our goals.

The need for quantitative measurement associated with the current accountability craze allowed me to better understand my own schooling and my expected role as an educator. As a result of school factors, the neighborhood elements, and a hidden curriculum—a curriculum not taught but implicitly part of what is experienced and expected of students—students' learning is often misrepresented through quantification and outside high-stakes-testing benchmarks. These issues affect how students are educated and how the specific curriculum is presented. Jean Anyon's (1980) critical ethnographic study of different classrooms in varying socioeconomic environments raises important issues I struggled with every day. In the study, Anyon showed that students taught in such ways that they were either expected to exceed expectations, show creative problem solving, follow rules, give already known answers, or even fail often live up to these expectations. Depending on students' socioeconomic status, the overwhelming contextual issues drive a perpetual notion regarding how a student is perceived to be successful. Interestingly, students, along with their teacher, are attuned to issues of their environment or community, and together are expected to conform. Intrigued by Anyon's inquiry, I wanted to challenge her disparaging findings regarding the low expectations with my own students.

As a product of a professional-class education, I was taught to be creative and question. This ingrained ideal was not only truncated for my students of a lower socioeconomic class but also affected me as an educator. Unfortunately, my classroom was expected to be an environment where the curriculum was an element of cultural reproduction—where the norms and values of a particular group's previous generations are repeated. It was to be a place where the status quo was perpetuated and salient knowledge reproduced. The curriculum itself and the way it is taught are often driving forces responsible for gross inequities that advance the unjust socioeconomic stratification in this country.

Despite the dedicated Carr educators, students had often been taught in ways that may have furthered these inequities. I wondered if it would be a service to introduce them to educational experiences similar to those I had had in school. I realized I had had considerable opportunities when growing up, but I needed to examine issues of race and imposition to better understand how I wanted to run my classroom. As a White teacher in a school with all African American students, I understood that race, class, and privilege did matter. Simply entering a classroom serving Cabrini Green had implications regarding power and control, and the ways students perceived the dynamic were important.

I wanted to be innovative and allow the students to be creative, but the societal pressures—like "back to the basics," "teaching to the test," and "adequate yearly progress"—hindered my autonomy and freedom and, in turn, my students' learning. I was expected to teach to standardized achievement tests and deliver scripted, content-based lesson plans. Although the canned materials were presented as best practices, they were clearly not effective ways to reach my students. From in-service workshops to formulas for teaching specific subject matter, I often felt shackled, not allowed to think and theorize for myself. Impacting this issue was the fact that lower socioeconomic classes, especially Black children from public housing, are not given the choices and freedoms accorded to those in more affluent areas. The accepted prescription for success for my students was to follow the rules so that they could achieve a prescribed outcome, typically measured by their test scores, that destined them to remain in the same low-income environment and socioeconomic class.

When I interviewed at Carr, innovation was stressed. Being a new teacher with a diverse educational background, I thought I had many answers to the creativity issues presented and would be able to act on them based on previous experiences. Soon after accepting the position, I was alarmed that the real priority appeared to be achieving the goals set by the omnipotent board of education. This was far from the nurturing outlet advertised; I realized that the "creative goals" were based on test scores. I did not realize before accepting the position that children of different socioeconomic classes are taught differently, with an expectation of equity while lacking a foundation of equity. My struggle as an educator went from attempting to provide the innovative space I had anticipated to manipulating the environment to enable us, a White teacher and a classroom of African American students, to express ourselves more freely within this prescribed curriculum.

Fortunately, my license to be creative was not denied, but extreme daily pressure to achieve according to standards was imposed on me through outside mandates. From the beginning, I struggled with how to empower my students while simultaneously respecting a principal who was pressured by looming probationary threats based on (predetermined) academic achievement. My concern was that the goal of (inequitable) education might hinder students' progress and even perpetuate more inequity in their future. Was it better for my students to be aware of their potential through more democratic curricula, or was this questioning going to create more of a struggle for them in their future? Was I acting as an instrument of the dominant culture, or was I able to cut through this power dynamic to reach my students?

Part of my teaching philosophy was to let students see their own potential and challenge the socioeconomic designations governing the way they were to learn and be taught. Who was I to come into their world and teach them the way I thought they ought to be taught? How would insiders and outsiders perceive it? I wanted my students to succeed, to achieve, and to have endless possibilities in their lives through education. I was also forced to reconcile my own identity in the midst of trying to understand the realities of students' lives outside of school and meet their needs. I had grave concerns that my ideals of progressive education in this particular school might set up failures in the students' futures based on their predetermined educational road for success. Should the teacher challenge the preexisting societal norms in education? I wondered if my students would challenge the validity of their prescribed education only to find themselves running in place. Would a democratic curriculum empower or disable my classroom? Ultimately, could education change the social hierarchy? What would happen if I really provided a space in the classroom to allow for the images of education advocated by John Dewey, L. Thomas Hopkins, Paulo Freire, and Joseph Schwab over the past hundred years?

Intrigued by these philosophers' ideas, I wanted to incorporate their theories into my classroom. By embracing the students' interests, needs, and desires, we could make meaning from our shared experience. I questioned the appropriateness of the idea that children were taught in a certain way depending on their social class and believed they deserved something better. I also challenged my own idea that teachers were expected to teach varying social classes of students in these different ways.

Through their class project, the students from Cabrini Green were given the opportunity and responsibility to be active participants in the development and design of their learning. They all were critical participants in their learning and embraced the idea to co-create their curriculum. Like their peers in more affluent schools, Carr students—expected to follow the rules and give the right answers—were provided the space to problem-pose, challenge, and deliberate. They discovered ways of making their own interpretations by focusing on understanding and exploration rather than on absolute, prescriptive truths. Contrary to the education so common and expected in urban public schools, this approach allowed us to realize that they had strengths and aptitudes no authorities expected them to have in school. Instead of being conceived as mere vessels to be filled with knowledge, they were challenged to create their own knowledge by theorizing with one another and me.

In a cultural environment that typically does not reward the untaught curricula, and where out-of-school, null, and nonschool curricula are not acknowledged or rewarded, my students discovered ways to bridge the gap. There was no artificial break to change subjects since curricular problems were inherently interconnected. The naturalistic approach to solving their issues allowed learning to emerge through their own lived experience. This phenomenological learning rewarded their knowledge and resisted the urge of educators to provide "the capital K knowledge" so often promoted in schools, especially those serving poor or working-class students. I learned that content and objectives can come from the students. Just as students in the more affluent schools are encouraged and rewarded for their insight and creativity, these low-income, urban, African American students now had their voices heard.

As Ralph Nader (2004c) proclaimed on a visit to our classroom:

Prepar[ing] for the tests, turn[ing] the curriculum to the test . . . distorts the curriculum. This is just the opposite. You are engaged in a very important experiment, which is succeeding. This is going to get known all over the country because you are doing better on these tests, not by preparing for these tests . . . but by developing a real learning process . . . you are going to turn some theories upside down!

Instead of "turn[ing] some theories upside down," this curricular approach actually embraced what the revered educational thinkers provided in their theoretical guidance. Putting their theories into purposeful action, my students and I were able to see that when we developed learning in such a way that everyone had an active role in problem solving, we were successful together.

EDUCATION AS A TWO-WAY STREET

Part of my interest in creating an experientially based classroom with students is a direct result of my own experiences in elementary school, middle-level grades, and high school.

I attended a neighborhood public elementary school a short walk through modest cookie-cutter-subdivision homes in a Cleveland suburb.

The homogeneous student population received a typical suburban education. Class sizes were not unreasonable. Teachers were generally approach-
able. Most parents didn't question their children's education. Content was
prepackaged in basal textbooks provided by the district. And the school
rarely had any controversy.

The prospects of junior and senior high school in the community were
not as promising. Because these schools were large and overcrowded, with
the reputation that teachers did not care about student achievement or
success, my parents sought an alternative for the remainder of my forma-
tive years.

University School, an all-boys, college preparatory, country day school,
was vastly different from the local elementary school. The student population was predominantly from the professional and elite class. Although
many students came from privilege, the school embraced diversity and
sought out students from differing backgrounds, ethnicities, and cultures
(although this goal was secondary to fulfilling the needs of the city's most
affluent families).

Classrooms were stocked with limitless resources for inquiry-based
learning. Teachers, many experts in their fields, were encouraged to develop innovative strategies using state-of-the-art materials. The school's
hundred-year history championed a core curriculum to nurture future leaders and community servants, while also providing opportunities for the
boys to pursue their own interests. This approach caused me to question
the previous scripted, boring lessons. School was no longer the fact-based
memorization, rote learning, and regurgitation I had become comfortable
with during my grade-school years. Rather than compartmentalized subjects, the coursework combined disciplinary subjects into seamless, the-
matic endeavors.

The school's experiential classrooms provided for learning with real
parts and real consequences. Examining the results of our efforts became
real-life assessments, while written testing played only a minor role. Teachers acted as facilitators. Our understanding was evaluated by how well we
understood problems and ultimately through our results in solving them.
Outcomes were often unknown prior to exploration, and students usually
worked in tandem with teachers to investigate predicaments presented.

These sorts of interdisciplinary curricular initiatives had a lasting effect on me and would inevitably resurface in my own classroom. Realizing that the opportunities from my experiences were not only privileged
but also unique and rarely attempted in public education, I wondered if

this approach could be replicated in Cabrini Green. Although Carr did not have the resources or environment of my schooling, there were still authentic elements that could be examined. It seemed possible to challenge the curricular norms of urban public schools if the classroom could focus on real issues rather than prescriptive ones. Could some attributes of my elite education be emulated in a school serving a public housing project?

After these engaging activities at University School, lecture-style classes during college were often disappointing. Not until my last semester did I find myself in a class centering on the student. Deeply rooted in experiential learning and the psychology of flow (Csikszentmihalyi, 1990)—a time at which skills and challenges meet when people report feelings of extreme concentration and deep enjoyment—the class sparked my interest in investigating different forms successful learning can take while striving to meet the needs of individuals.

Following this turning point in my own education, various teaching and learning opportunities further grounded this vocation. From teaching at the university level, to guiding groups in adventure education and Outward Bound expeditionary learning, to corporate consulting in an educational capacity, I realized that I had found flow. Through a guiding mentor, I learned to structure coursework experientially and discovered that students often derive the greatest benefit when their progress is self-directed—something reminiscent of the University School teaching methods.

After several years of corporate consulting, I left to teach at William D. Carr Community Academy. Located amid the high-rise tenements of Chicago's Cabrini Green housing project, the school was quite a change from a top-floor office in a downtown skyscraper—although just blocks apart. Anticipating that students at Carr might lack motivation for traditional education similar to what I had experienced in my elementary days, I envisioned an opportunity to apply hands-on learning in my classroom.

Despite having dreams of making my classroom an experiential haven, when I actually entered the school on the first day, I realized teaching was much more difficult and complex than I had anticipated. After the first few days, I was not sure I would make it. More than once I contemplated quitting and never returning. The students knew how to push my buttons, and they tested me to see if I had what it took to endure life at Carr Academy.

Teaching (and learning) with my class at Carr was unlike anything I had ever encountered. I realized that if I was not going to leave, I had to figure out a way to "be the boss." I needed to take authority and tell the students what I expected by laying down the law! Even though this was not how I had pictured myself in the role as teacher, I saw this as the only option. It was my responsibility to educate the children, and as frustrated as I was in this capacity, I readily examined the basal textbooks for anything to keep my students busy. This was hardly emulating the problem-based, cooperative learning curriculum I wanted to create, but at the time there was no alternative.

After I got more comfortable teaching, I began experimenting with the vision of how my classroom could be constructed. I realized I did not always have to be the dominant classroom voice and could share authority with students. By giving students opportunities to help run the classroom activities, I would be more respected, and the days would not be nearly as long.

Although these first steps in my progressive teaching methods often failed miserably, I can reflect back and see some inappropriateness in my early incarnations. That first school year was all about trial and error. I was certainly learning about what it meant to teach, even though I came in confident that I already knew it all. My arrogance faded quickly. I discovered how challenging teaching was, especially teaching students with different life experiences from my own.

In the beginning, I exuded all the power I could, and in the end my goal was markedly different: to try to make the classroom revolve around the students. The transition from being authoritative to sharing control is comical to me now. My first attempt at a student-centered education was making my fifth graders responsible for what they were learning by creating a syllabus for the quarter and informing the students what was expected. The self-motivated succeeded and moved rapidly ahead of the rest of the class, while the majority of my 27 charges struggled without guidance. It was apparent I did not yet fully understand my role or my place in my own classroom.

As time went on, I began to get more creative, and realized that I could learn from my students rather than always being the keeper of the knowledge. Students started to take control of their own learning, and education became a two-way street. An important aspect of this type of interest-based learning was allowing the students to pick any topic and generate questions associated with it.

I allowed a student who was interested in basketball to brainstorm questions related to this topic. Questions about current players, averages, and other statistics led to other questions that delved deep into history and social concerns about the sport. Similarly, one student's interest in hip-hop music led him to the Harlem Renaissance. Becoming a fifth-grade expert in this African American cultural movement, he was able to answer a multitude of classmates' questions and share insights with them.

Students flourished with these sorts of projects. They enjoyed the opportunity to study topics they deemed worthwhile. Students' questions broke down barriers of compartmentalization typical to disciplines of knowledge. This broadening of subject matter provided some of the educational strategies used in my own private school education. Although I did not yet know how to facilitate these miniprojects, perhaps, I thought, something was brewing that could transcend the disengaging textbook.

Before my first year of teaching had ended, I stepped out of my comfort zone to allow my students to explore their community and themselves. This last project encouraged students to use multimedia to portray their lives after school. This could be unique to each child and have endless possibilities. This project had multiple purposes: I could learn about students as individuals, I could get a view of the daily experiences they had that were different from my own, and the students could become engaged and motivated by a fun activity about their own lives. Seeking to be a student of my students, I also vowed to participate alongside them. While the rest of Carr's student body had given up on schoolwork after the month of standardized testing, my students went into overdrive as they embraced the student-directed opportunity. The school year ended on this high note, and I was excited about the possibility of new curriculum projects for the upcoming year.

During the summer as a doctoral student at the University of Illinois at Chicago, I was continuously exposed to invaluable curriculum studies literature. This reading helped me shape a classroom where the students could really be self-directed and centered on their concerns. Exposing myself to literature about progressive education and the practical curriculum orientation, I set out to create this space.

Reflecting on how one curriculum theorizer, Joseph Schwab (1978), asserted that curriculum based on generalizations and theory alone was unacceptable and needed purposeful construction for involved participants, I altered my teaching approach. Schwab saw curriculum development as deliberative, mediated by the commonplaces of education: students, teachers, subject matter, and milieu. I strove to create a classroom that valued this at its foundation. Although many educators saw Schwab's argument as a rejection of theory, I thought it readily applied to my teaching.

Schwab contended that for deliberative processes between all stake-holders to be meaningful and worthwhile, a practical approach to curriculum is necessary to meet the situational needs of students. By emphasizing a plurality and multiplicity of theories and practices (rather than the common focus on a theory alone or the latest trend), I could differentiate and nurture individuals based on particular needs in given situations. Utilizing this perspective provided a vehicle for my classroom to integrate instruction authentically.

Realizing the Internet could be a powerful tool to tailor instruction for each student, I convinced my principal to allow the class to meet in the school's technology lab during our mandated reading time each day. With his permission for the lab usage, and the awarding of multiple grants to bring technology resources into the lives of my students (wireless laptops, word processors, digital cameras, and digital video equipment), I was able to bridge the digital divide in a school that was severely underresourced.

Many schools that have such infrastructure inadequacies could not realize the luxury of this technology, but in this case the students were afforded access to technology not only in the classroom but at home as well. This led to the conceptualization of a model that would focus on the students' priorities and interests while at the same time addressing achievement gaps.

To do so, I developed a student-directed approach, coupled with pertinent feedback via a Web-based resource called the Northwestern University Collaboratory Project. The Collaboratory Project is an initiative sponsored by Northwestern University that provides training, technological services, and resources to assist teachers and students in developing Web-based projects and activities. The kid-friendly, free-of-charge technology helps to further educational achievement in a collaborative and secure Internet environment (http://collaboratory.nunet.net). Together, we deliberated and discovered what was most worthwhile for our learning. The Collaboratory environment and the technology resources provided a means to avoid making curriculum generalizations, thus enabling me to focus on each student. A model evolved to create practical inquiry in my classroom.

Because the Collaboratory project was able to be accessed online, the emergent project allowed Carr elementary students to be linked with graduate student mentors from a university over 700 miles away via the Internet. Using the Collaboratory's interactive Web-based approach, these fifth graders pursued their own interests through writing, while receiving individualized comments from doctoral students studying literacy. The feedback helped students create multiple drafts and improve their writing skills over time.

Realistically, I could not offer daily, individualized feedback to each student, but this mentor model could. This was key because the spectrum of reading levels in my classroom was vast. Students worked at their own pace, not affected by peers' progress or limitations. With constant guidance and scaffolding, the writing dyads created and met purposeful, unique achievement goals. Students were inspired, eager to write for their mentor and for themselves. Concurrently, graduate students were afforded opportunities to develop skills working with children. Just as I was learning from my fifth graders, the doctoral students learned from and with their fifth-grade counterparts. Everyone realized the luxury of the individualized and student-specific feedback. Excited by the project, my students wrote and took pride in their daily work by utilizing this technology-driven mentor model. My students were motivated because they realized they had an authentic audience—real people genuinely interested in their work. Their writing now had purpose. As one fifth grader commented, "It is so great to have somebody help me get all the ideas out of my head and written down without my teacher's red pen on my paper." This ongoing project certainly made the students more confident and higher achievers, instilling the value of their work and reasons to constantly improve.

As this comprehensive project linked many subject areas, diversity and equity were also important project elements and were achieved by linking graduate students from the rural South with elementary students from urban Chicago. The ongoing communication facilitated inquiry by both groups into cultural differences. Effective forms of communication were addressed through writing, and the corresponding discourse highlighted similarities and differences between the groups. This model was significant in several aspects, as it stressed the need for individualized curriculum and created a model for higher education students to act as mentors and to assist classroom teachers. In addition, it provided practical and applied use of theory. This Collaboratory mentor model was a springboard for other initiatives, and the skills acquired were readily transferable, influencing my students beyond this particular experience.

Now that the students realized that their voices counted, I was ready to take the curriculum one step further. But how could I keep pushing students while meeting the standards that were advertised daily as the imperative to be accomplished? My teaching was transforming, but I was still looking for opportunities to provide space for my students to excel, realize their abilities, and use their talents to help themselves. Because I had come to realize that what they had to say was not only important but also enlightening, I knew their ideas needed to be heard.

2

Our School Is a Dump!
Identifying a Problem
That Needs Solving

THIS AIN'T NO SCHOOLWORK, THIS IS IMPORTANT!

I scanned the room thinking that this was going to be another professional development workshop where I would be continually glancing at the clock, wondering when the session would end. The beginning of the new school year had already been filled with teacher training that left me frustrated and uninspired, and I thought this seminar would be like the others. Surprisingly, as I sat in the back, I realized how invigorating the topic of this workshop could be for my students and me.

This education workshop was on Project Citizen, a program that promotes citizenship in the schools. It detailed a way to get fifth- through eighth-grade students involved in public policy. By tackling an identified problem, students would learn how to implement change. After reading about inquiry-based teaching and progressive education, I saw the Project Citizen agenda as a way to achieve student-directed learning in the classroom, where teachers and students could work together to create a meaningful curriculum. Ideally, it could enable students to engage in an authentic activity of their choosing that crossed disciplinary boundaries and where subjects became complementary and integrated.

The workshop presenters suggested that students identify a simple problem in their school or community. Examples ranged from fixing cracked sidewalks at a nearby park to getting the school administration to mandate recess every day. I believed my students could become more passionate if they chose a problem that was important to them. The problem needed to be theirs, not mine. The Project Citizen coordinators cautioned teachers to keep the project within the school. This "think small" advocacy made some sense: It would allow teachers to easily manage the project, thereby steering it within the prescribed guidelines.

I had high hopes for implementing Project Citizen. I saw it as a chance to develop something with students to further their interest without limits. Not looking to impose ideas or parameters, I wanted students to determine what was a worthwhile project. During the workshop. I tried to conceptualize what could be. The students could choose a topic that would really raise their level of confidence in the classroom and demonstrate their talent and ability. My students problem-solved outside of the classroom in their neighborhood on a daily basis. The unfortunate part was that the school setting did not recognize these problem-solving or critical thinking skills. I wanted to find a way to bring these street-savvy, analytic qualities into the classroom.

After the seminar, I wrote in my journal:

> This could be the opportunity I have longed for. What students choose is not relevant, although I hope it is bigger than a school issue . . . perhaps a larger societal or community problem could use their energy and will make them feel charged and empowered.

The Project Citizen curriculum idea would be a perfect opportunity to push my students. I continued journaling, "I wonder if they can motivate themselves to a greater good and strive for higher moral ground as a result of the project." I wanted to take the curriculum away from scripted lesson plans and give it to the students to develop their unique interests.

Following the seminar, I invited the lead coordinator from the Constitutional Rights Foundation Chicago (CRFC), the local sponsor of Project Citizen, to visit Carr and present an introductory lesson on public policy.

Just after the Thanksgiving holiday, the CRFC coordinator arrived at Carr with some critical thinking exercises that allowed the students to become actively involved solving realistic problems that kids faced in schools. Although the fifth graders appeared interested in the challenges, none of us realized how extensive the efforts of these 10- to 12-year-old students would become once they focused on their own problem. Several days later, the coordinator e-mailed that she "was charmed by the kids and wants to highlight them in a story for the organization's newsletter sent to 20,000 people." I decided that the decision about whether to allow her to feature our classroom should include the students.

Allowing students decision-making authority became a recurring theme in our classroom. Did they want to remain low-key, or did they want to get some publicity about their ideas? With winter break fast approaching, there was limited time to begin focusing on the project. After I told the students about the possibility of being featured, they were keen to begin.

Identifying the Problem

The next day students chose to participate in one of two groups, either with the gym teacher who came into our classroom each day to assist during reading time or with me, to brainstorm potential problems worth trying to solve. Both of us encouraged the students to generate a list of as many issues as possible.

With my group, I wrote down the ideas that were being suggested. As the ideas came out of their mouths, I quickly divided the suggestions into distinct categories: school issues, neighborhood issues, and societal problems. The kids were eager to see the list as it was being created. Everyone wanted a shot at coming up with the next cool idea that would spark interest in a peer sitting nearby. Even though there was a lot of excitement, the kids quieted each other so the other group would not hear them, set on generating the most original problems in their self-made competition.

After approximately an hour of brainstorming, we regrouped. While the lists were read, everyone was quite attentive. When items were repeated, the class commented. At one point a student shouted, "We said it first . . . you copied off of us." As more problems were cited, another student frustratedly said, "We hearin' the same things over and over," but I did not see it the same way. Certainly, a student may have mentioned the "bathrooms are messed up 'cause the toilets don't work" while another cited "leaky sinks in the restrooms." Although the kids thought they were the same issues, they were distinct elements of a bigger problem. As I tried to defuse the arguing, Dyneisha made her emphatic point about the school being the problem.

Dyneisha's proclamation that "Our school is a dump" caused chaos in the classroom. Students were shouting, "My school sucks," "It's a dump," and "We need a brand-new one" as they ran around the room. Looking back to the 89 different problems students named, approximately 30 of them dealt with the school's inadequacy. Although pleased with their selection, I had anticipated they would not have focused on such a loaded social issue but would have wanted something more immediate or tangible, for example, getting fruit punch at lunch or demanding free time at school every day.

Reflecting now on what occurred throughout the whole school year, this reaction troubles me. Was I surprised because I did not think my students had it in them? Was I thinking this was too big of an issue for students from Cabrini Green to handle? Whatever the initial inclination, these questions were in the back of my mind. My students were capable and diligent, but I always wondered about the origins of my reservations. My questioning brought up the problematic nature of race in the classroom. As a White, middle-class teacher entering a classroom in Cabrini Green, I was an admitted outsider, struggling with getting to know the students. I wanted to build relationships with the students, but at the same time my

Problems That Affect Our Community and Us

1. New windows
2. Better school lunch
3. Bigger school
4. Gym in building
5. Starting kids in the NBA
6. Full pad football
7. Bathroom stalls new
8. New nurses
9. Psychiatrist
10. More teachers
11. More security
12. No library
13. New tables
14. New desks
15. Security cameras
16. No failing
17. Carpet floors
18. Bigger rooms
19. New closets
20. Nicer rooms
21. More aides
22. Can bring food to school
23. Get out earlier
24. Dry erase boards
25. New computers
26. More computers
27. More specials
28. Recess every day
29. Add high school
30. Lunchroom
31. More dollars for school
32. Fewer games
33. Better security
34. No wars
35. More community service
36. Better police
37. More sports
38. Safer neighborhoods
39. More garbagemen
40. Better public high schools
41. More fancy buildings
42. More hotels
43. More parks
44. Better maps
45. 2 presidents
46. Another president
47. Kid mayors
48. Kids day
49. Kid president
50. Bulletproof vests for kids
51. Better houses
52. More schools for the handicapped
53. Stop violence
54. Stop rage
55. Stop fighting
56. Faster police cars
57. Fewer days of school
58. Lower travel costs
59. Build a bridge over Lake Michigan
60. Make gas free
61. Cheaper cars
62. Fix the heat in the building
63. Get AC
64. Get a whole new building
65. Fix the school up and make it nice
66. No big trucks on the expressway
67. Better drivers
68. One lane for cars and one lane for trucks
69. Trade places with the rich people
70. Black president
71. More Black leaders
72. Home for the homeless
73. Help for the poor
74. $1 a day for the homeless
75. Food for the poor
76. Free prosthetics
77. Clothes for the homeless
78. Better car windows
79. Need an auditorium
80. Better windows at school
81. Cafeteria at school
82. Choice of food at school
83. New bathrooms
84. New drinking fountains
85. Get rid of gangs
86. Get rid of hypes and drugs
87. No more stalkers and rapermen
88. Too much littering and trash
89. Stop Michael Jackson

feelings made me question my actions and authority. Although I had the best intentions for my students, was I giving them what they needed to succeed, or was I creating a potential problem? If the students were given permission to problem-pose and question the curriculum, would this create future conflicts in school?

The discussion continued. Intent on making their complaints loud and clear, the students forced me to wrestle with what was acceptable and what crossed the line in the classroom, as some of the problems focused on teachers they wanted fired. Getting the topic shifted away from personnel issues wasn't easy. I wanted to share authority with students but saw the need to remain in charge. I was afraid of what might happen if I gave them too much freedom. Could it get so out of hand that I wouldn't be able to regain the classroom control a teacher should have? Rather than dwelling on the problematic personnel talk, I instead encouraged students whose ideas focused on the problems with the school building to elaborate.

As the discussion was redirected, 12 distinct subtopics emerged. The categories of school building problems took on their own identities through vivid descriptions, and the kids were already trying to come up with solutions! This was a bizarre predicament; eventually, we would need to come up with solutions, but now I had to persuade them away from that step so as not to lose focus on the problems themselves.

As I jotted down the long list of bathroom symptoms, a colleague appeared at the door to take out some kids for special help in reading. Mesmerized by the room's intensity, he was drawn in. He commented, "I have never seen you guys so excited about schoolwork." And a quick reply was snapped back at him, "This ain't no schoolwork, this is important!" This revelation supported what I had striven for since I began teaching. How could students be engaged in something creative that they wanted to participate in, rather than feel they were being forced? The boys normally taken for special reading instruction, typically quiet in the classroom, were now active participants. These boys, along with all of their peers, knew more about the building's shortcomings than anyone else. The activity was leveraging something they already knew, and they demonstrated their sophisticated knowledge.

Moving to the Next Stage

With so much excitement in the classroom, I needed to keep up the momentum. I had an idea, but it was problematic. Recognizing the great work the coordinator from CRFC had done with the students on her initial visit, I wanted to invite her back for a follow-up lesson. Students could present their findings to her. I felt she was a safe audience and could guide us to our next steps. The problem was inviting another young White figure as an "expert" into the classroom once again. Because I myself was struggling to relate to my students' culture, I realized another outsider's presence in the classroom was not going to help me get closer to what my students were experiencing in or out of school. I was a teacher in this dilapidated school, but both the coordinator and I had a choice in being at Carr. Would her presence in the classroom cast her as the White woman with "expert knowledge" on solving *their* problem?

As I struggled with proceeding, I cautiously brought my issue to the students. Not really knowing how they would respond, I asked for their input. I had heard a student's comment after her first visit: "She don't know what we be going through here." Struggling with my desire to pretend that this did not occur, I realized that ignoring the racial differences would not help the issue, but addressing it was uncomfortable. I worried about how our differences could affect the classroom. After some discussion, the class decided to have her back following winter vacation. The students believed she could help them reach a larger audience; they wanted her to gather direct quotes and pictures for her newsletter.

During winter break, I took the time to gain perspective on how I could make the classroom a place that ensured student-directed learning with a renewed sense of purpose in my teaching. It also provided an opportunity to think about how this classroom curriculum could meet the expectations and prescriptions from outside mandates.

After break, I assigned the students to each write about the problem they had identified. After I had given a writing prompt, several students asked if they could also take photographs to visually show the problem. Throughout the month of January, the class began documenting the problems in the school through photography and expository essays about its shortcomings. The students' compositions were astonishingly sophisticated. When asked how they were able to construct such amazing rough drafts, Demetrius responded, "This stuff is really important, and I need to get the word out if I want something done." These rough drafts became a turning point; getting the word out is exactly what they accomplished. An example of one student's uncorrected first draft demonstrated how intentional students were about exposing the school's problems:

Our school building William D Carr Academy has big problems. These three main ideas are what I think are important issues: restrooms, temperature and windows. . . .

The restrooms are filthy and dirty. There are spitballs all over the place. They do not get cleaned up properly. It is also really smelly in the bathrooms. As an example of how bad they are, sinks move and water leaks on the floor. The sinks have bugs in them and water is everywhere. The hot water faucets have cold water. Kids don't like using the bathrooms since they are so gross and falling apart. . . .

The heat is not turned on. It is really cold in the classrooms. As another example we have to put on our coats during class because it is so cold. They cannot fix it because the pipes are broken. It is uncomfortable and hard to learn. Our hands are cold and we cannot write. This needs to be changed.

As another example the windows are cracked. It is cold in our class because the windows are cracked. There are bullet holes in the windows. The windows are not efficient enough. We can not see through the windows. There is tape on the windows. It is dark in the classrooms. We can not hardly see what we are doing because it is so dark.

You should come here and see for yourself. You would not let your kids come to a school that is falling apart. Since windows, tempature and restrooms are not right we should get a whole new school building. The problems are not fixable.

All the students produced similar work. Proving their capabilities in a worthwhile cause, the students not only had something well written to submit; they also convincingly presented the issues of school inequity they faced every day. They were not afraid to describe the situation as they saw it, and they were ready and willing to ask for change. Each student's expository representation of the school's problems was written as a "come see for yourself" piece. Essentially, they guided themselves to the next step in the process.

Class time was well spent, with students reading their text aloud. Usually, students feared reading out loud; however, in this case each child fought for the opportunity to share his or her prose. Many had already received feedback from their online writing mentors in the Collaboratory Project and felt confident not only in the accuracy of their syntax but also in the writing quality. This was a noticeably positive experience for Room 405 students.

Fortunately, within days following the coordinator's second visit, she e-mailed the article for the *Constitutional Rights Foundation Chicago Legal Circle* newsletter. I planned to use her article as part of the class's reading time and printed copies for each student. Before we could even begin to read the text and try to understand its meaning, the stack of paper was snatched from my hands by two girls in the class.

There were two photos included as part of the article, and the moment the girls caught a glimpse of themselves in the paper they were ecstatic. I remember hearing them run to show their classmates, boasting, "Check it out, we can see ourselves in d'news." When the others noticed that only three of their peers' photographs were included in the newsletter, they were palpably disappointed that, as they put it, "Our mugs didn't make the cut." Overall, however, they were still elated that the story of the class was published.

The excitement around the first written testament of their blossoming efforts allowed me to use text about them for our language arts time. The students were able to read, outline, deconstruct, and analyze the story, "Project Citizen at Carr Academy: Fifth Graders Tackle a Big Problem," written by the coordinator about the work they were doing (Chethik, 2004).

This major step in "getting the word out" gave students a sense of confidence and made them more determined to proceed. As we read through the document together, the students were on the edges of their seats, totally engaged. Even though they helped to write the article, gave some quotes, and talked about their work, it was surreal for them to read about what they had already done as a group. Unlike most accounts they had previously read about their community, which focused on pathology and despair, the students were being highlighted for their work. This article was different; it was a testament to them and their potential.

As we continued reading through the article, students commented about its accuracy and perspective. Questions were raised "'bout why she didn't tell this part?" It was a great opportunity to discuss media representation and examine written perspective in the way news gets communicated. Together we asked questions about why the piece detailed certain ideas more than others and, as a result, discussed how others represent events and activities. The important part to me was that Cabrini Green students' brave efforts were portrayed in a hopeful way.

FEELIN' LIKE A BIG AND POWERFUL GROWN-UP

Although complaining about the condition of the school continued, students were not taking any action, and we were already in the first week of February. Certainly I had ideas for the project's direction, but I wanted the students to be more decisive. If I got too involved, would it taint the student-directed project? As both the teacher and a group member who had expertise, I was presented with the tension between being democratic and pedagogic.

Several class periods were spent doing preliminary research to better understand local government and see who was running the show. Several students realized that we needed the support of both the local administration and the Local School Council (LSC). One student suggested we could interview his uncle, a Local School Council representative. Another student offered to talk to the alderman. A third informed the class he knew the Illinois Secretary of State from his local tumbling team. They all had great ideas and seemed eager enough to get the ball rolling, but nothing happened—nothing. Due to the initial interest, time for Project Citizen was built into the school day. The students offered ideas, but no one was acting on them. The project seemed to be faltering.

After several days, Tyrone, a quiet boy, finally got the courage to approach another teacher who was a Local School Council member for an interview. At last, somebody was taking action!

Tyrone met with the teacher, returning with several pages of notes based on an interview template he had pulled from his Project Citizen workbook. Tyrone gave an impromptu presentation to the class:

> I interviewed Mr. Wurtzman because he is on the LSC. He told me everyone got a responsibility to make the community better . . . and believes we should have a new school because the school has parts that ain't safe. . . . If we want a new school we should tell the parents to have more meetings in the community. . . . And, he feels the capital improvement program are trying to get the new school but gave the money away quick. State government needs to pay more so all districts could get better schools. . . . For more information ask the alderman or Reverend Tinter, the LSC president.

According to my notes taken during his talk, "Tyrone did an excellent job, but seemed a little embarrassed. I was praising him since he had taken action and did not just talk about what he wanted to do. His class-mates also gave him props."

Later that day, as we were heading back from the gym, the LSC president was leaving the school office. On seeing him, several students ran up to him, requesting an interview. As they turned to me for guidance, I redirected them to figure out when, where, and how on their own. They scheduled an interview the next day, but before he left, Jaris showed the LSC president some of the class's work. He was immediately interested, requesting copies of all the documents.

Considering Project Citizen

The following morning, prior to the LSC president's afternoon visit, I felt it was finally time to formally ask the students how they felt about working with Project Citizen. I am not sure I picked the most opportune time; the students were especially noisy and it was freezing cold. Earlier, we had read the thermometer and plotted the classroom temperature on a graph. The 9:00 A.M. temperature was 59°, a significant change from the previous day's reading of almost 80°. The temperature fluctuated so much it was hard to predict the room conditions. On some days classroom windows were cranked open to let in the February freeze, while on others, students wore hats, gloves, and coats. One student said it best, "The temperature be broken!" Another commented, "It is hard to work when it is so cold, my fingers hurt and I have to wear my mittens; you know it ain't easy to write with mittens."

Although most kids were working, several disturbances, including flatulent sounds, provoked giggles from the group. Despite not having their full attention, I began a somewhat serious discussion on the issues related to Project Citizen. Students talked about how they really liked the choices and freedom the project allowed. As more students got involved in the discussion, the disruptions dissipated. After suggesting things to think about, we headed to the computer lab, where students could respond in their online journals.

Walking down the hall, the students talked quietly with one another. There was no line, something that was never a priority for me as a teacher. I was always curious about why teachers were so concerned with having their students march down the halls in a militaristic fashion. I always believed that students, as long as they did not disturb other classrooms, could make their way to their destination without the struggle of "the one person per tile" mentality commonly seen in the school hallways. Whether my class's lack of a line was due to my inability to make it happen or the fact that I didn't see the point, I enjoyed the conversation with students in the halls.

By changing the venue from the disruptive, uncomfortable classroom, I believed we could alter the dynamic so that everyone would participate. I was hopeful that the students could capture the essence of the discussion in their writing. Moving to the computer lab might also allow everyone the opportunity to respond to one another.

After I reminded them of where to find their online journals, most students started writing without hesitation. The joking and talking of several minutes earlier subsided, and they seemed intent on expressing their feelings about Project Citizen. I repeated the broad prompt from the classroom, encouraging the students to free-write, which had always been difficult for them.

Typically, when students were asked to write without specific direction, the results were not exemplary and showed little effort. I wanted their raw emotions revealed in the writing rather than prescribed texts that would all sound the same. Stepping over dangling cords as I made my way around the computers, I caught a glimpse of their writing while trying to go unnoticed. They were aggressively attacking the keyboards as they wrote both quantity and quality. These journal entries were different from prior work not focused on their interests. Their enthusiasm was apparent in each entry.

The students were readily able to make sense of and theorize about what was occurring. Their writing demonstrated how engaged they were in choosing how and what to do with the Project Citizen efforts. The following excerpts, including language, spelling, and grammar errors from student journal entries, represent the class's feelings about the prospects of the project after about one month of work. Jaris wrote:

> project citizen is the best project I did all this year because I get to fight for what I belive in. I think this is the best project becasue I do not have to do what the techer want to do. . . .
>
> kids get to say what they feel and what they think. And that is great because most techer get to tell what the kids got to do and how to do it.
>
> I am really excited because if we get the CPS [Chicago Public Schools] and the CIP [Capital Improvement Program] to build us a new

school while we on summer break. . . . We wont have to go to that school that looks old and dirty and out of shape. I wonder about the CPS and the CIP. I think they do not want to build us a new school.

Jaris was focused on the idea that teachers often tell kids what to do in school. What struck me were his ideas about fighting for what he believed in, while understanding that there were specific entities that could help get a new school. He obviously applied information from the class's research efforts.

Others also commented on similar ideas about classroom choice with curriculum designed around what students wanted to do. For instance, Tyrone stated, "I like the fact we can tell teachers what we want. My favorite part is that we can tell the teachers what they messed up and what they do wronge."

Tavon discussed reaching a wider audience and generating ideas from the students. Just as Jaris described his curiosity in how the decisions were made about the school, Tavon wrote on the prospects of influencing others:

We get to show people problems we think is important. Our classroom is doing a lot of interesting things like writing stories and interviewing people. . . . We have lots of problems with our school. If people come to our school from good schools and visit and did everything we did and ate lunch at our school they would not like it. . . . I feel that this is a really great program and that I can learn more by doing it.

Shaniqua saw connections between other classroom projects and discussed the student–teacher relationship. She raised the ideas of pride in the work they are doing. Her acknowledgment and awareness of what I had worked to cultivate with my students showed her understanding of classroom dynamics. Her comments illustrated how far I had come in my teaching practice. By my recognizing and building relationships through listening to the students' specific needs, the students and I could begin to connect. I found Shaniqua's discussion of her achievement through the project particularly intriguing:

I think we can keep doing this because it help you gooder and gooder and it makes my teacher happy and also make him proud of us. You also have to do alot of stuff in the project citizen but it help you do better. Room 405 will keep up the good work.

Other students also brought up the notion of pride. Dyneisha certainly was surprising herself when she described what the class was doing:

I really think this is a great thing that we are doing because it keep us out of the building and standing around while the gangbangres selling drugs. It's a good thing that my teacher has us doing this, but gusse what? He is not even telling us to do this. We took this big chance on are own and now we have to finsh it on are own . . . and we are.

The pride described by Dyneisha was evident in the writing of two students with individual education plans (IEPs). Both Kamala and Terrance were provided supplementary educational services. Fortunately, the classroom structure allowed them to fully participate and have their needs met through the project. They expressed how the Project Citizen curriculum made them active participants in their learning. Kamala wrote:

My favorite part of the project is that we could pick what we were going to do. My least favorite part about project citizen is thinking about it. I like doing it more than writeing it. Because I have a hard time concentrating when writeing rather than doing it. Project citizen lets me do a lot that I usualy cant. Being able to create this project makes me feel good to write.

Terrance commented:

We get to interview people on giving us information on getting a new school. This is cool because we have a choice to choose what we want and it helps me to understand. when kids get to create their own master plan on getting things done I believe that when that happens we can do better in school.

Terrance's point about students being able to construct their own "master plan" is priceless. The entries gave me insight into my students' thought processes. I used their writing to assist in my own critical reflection; it helped me theorize about how to continue. Although I recognized their investment, the journals allowed me to hear from them, in their own words, what made it so meaningful.

Conducting an Interview

Following the journaling, we returned to Room 405 for a discussion on conducting interviews. The class decided that everyone needed to be a part of the interview. We practiced by doing mock interviews to ready the group for the LSC president's anticipated arrival. We were able to role-play and practice. Everyone paid close attention as I modeled how to set up an interview and guided the interviewee's responses. The students demonstrated their attentiveness as the entire class fine-tuned their skills by asking practice questions and presenting scenarios.

Two boys set up a table in the center of the room and rehearsed, using the Project Citizen interview guides. Jaris took notes during our mock interviews so he could ask more pertinent probing questions of Reverend Tinter. Jaris even asked if he could talk about Blackness and if being Black was a reason why there was not a new school. I reiterated that everything was fair game, and they were in control of what they asked and how they asked it. Although I outwardly responded that the students could choose their questions, I privately had reservations about what they asked. I was uneasy about how someone who was not a classroom member—namely, the LSC president—might respond to the explicit questions about race, class, and privilege that were becoming more commonplace each day in Room 405. Would he think this kind of discussion was appropriate in a fifth-grade classroom? While the practice session continued, students deliberated, keenly focusing on what mattered to them in solving their problem.

The fact that Jaris wanted to bring up race as the reason for the school inequities showed how aware he was of the current school funding disparity for poor communities. Jaris demonstrated his ability to connect previous discussions with current issues in the neighborhood, exemplifying what needed to be addressed. Questions about racial discrimination were on students' minds, and the space provided allowed Room 405 to get closer to answering them. Raising the potentially politically controversial, racial-oriented concerns showed that Jaris and others were able to explore relevant topics that might have been considered taboo by many. In this case, the questions raised were not outside prompts but rather something the students wanted answered, and they were coming from within them. My journal revealed my thoughts about the interview:

Jaris really took charge and continued to be assertive, leaving behind his perpetual silliness. Tinter's message in the interview was convincing about involving others and being persistent. Believing the community deserved a new school, he emphatically responded to Jaris's question about race. Surprisingly, he did not believe it was because they were Black, arguing race shouldn't determine whether the kids get a school.

Even though I believe I understood his response, I could not help but think about the reasons the Cabrini community had not received the promised new building—reasons that had to do more with the neighborhood served and the complex relationship between race and class. The city and housing authority were in the midst of displacing African American families as they tore down the tenement buildings. With all the gentrification efforts, it was hard to separate the city and housing authority's message from what I observed. Although the public relations and popular media advertised that any family could transition into the new housing, the reality was that in my two years at Carr, only one family of a student in my classroom had had the opportunity to relocate into newly developed housing. From drug testing to requiring parental education, families needed to jump through hoops to even be considered in a lottery for new neighborhood housing. For too many, the process kept them away, and as a result many were being pushed out without alternatives.

Although somewhat cryptic about the race questions, Reverend Tinter was specific in encouraging a continuation of the discussion and possible next steps for the project: holding a press conference, getting Jesse Jackson and Rainbow/PUSH involved, and writing letters. Before he left the classroom, the students were noticeably invigorated and felt like they were gaining traction. Although he did not say anything out loud in the interview, suggestions made by Tinter, especially getting Jesse Jackson involved, implied that he, too, saw connections between the potential for a new school and complex race and class issues.

The following morning, Jaris documented from his notes what had occurred during the interview. Aside from the obvious answers about the need for a new school building, Jaris's subsequent reflection is evidence of how compelling the student curriculum was becoming:

When I interviewed Rev. Tinter I feel like I was a powerful person. I feel like I was a manger [manager] of a big time compony. Like I was the manger of a black program like Dr. king but the program I am in is to fight for a new school.

Usually in the class I do not feel powerful becuase everybody try to roast on me. But for the first time i felt powerful becuase i was interviewing a powerful person. It is a good thing becuase i never did this before. It is differnt kind of school. Usually kids do not interview grown ups. Grownups interview grownups. it made me feel like I was a big and powerful grownup. i think the interview will help us a lot becuase if we get more people to speak they will help us get a new school.

After the interview i started to run aorund and i was getting compliments from the teacher and students . . . i was the most important person in the class.

Jaris's journal entry revealed awareness of existing issues of power and privilege. This fifth grader's connections showed the potential in allowing students to co-create what and how they learn. His online journal was both astonishing and enlightening, showing that he understood what the expectations of children are and simultaneously was so uplifted by the power of the experience.

NEEDIN' THEM PIZZA THINGS

"How's we 'posed to get this new school?" students pointedly asked. Without answering, I asked them the same question. Did I return the question simply due to good teacher sense? Was it so they would have ownership? Or was I stalling? In reality, just like the students, I was questioning how to accomplish the feat, and I needed to learn from their insights.

As the teacher, I often felt like the ultimate authority in the eyes of the students. I often felt that if my authority was compromised, I was not doing my job. Beyond classroom management, I thought of authority in terms of content: I needed to know the answers to all questions posed. Wasn't it my role to solve everything from a disagreement to a math equation?

Finding myself in this complicated situation, I felt like I was letting the students down in my capacity as an educator by accepting questions I couldn't answer. For the first time as a teacher, I was on a more equal level to my students: Neither of us knew the potential outcome of our foray into politics. Just like the students, I did not know how to make this goal a reality.

The challenge by the LSC president to continue the fight was fresh in everyone's mind. Sitting in Carr's makeshift lunchroom in the third-floor corridor, the class was abuzz with what should happen next. Uplifted by the interview, we were anxious to develop the next steps for our impending battles.

Clearly, we were not solving a textbook problem. This was an authentic quest with real components, challenges, and obstacles. Triumph and tragedy would become part of our joint investigations. With much trepidation and humility, I revealed that I had never done anything like this before but was willing to give it my best shot with them. "We can only try and see what happens," I informed the fifth graders, emphasizing, "If we believe in what we are doing and we are fighting for what is right, all we can do is put our best foot forward." After coming to terms about my limited experience, I suggested we formulate a plan to accomplish the immense task.

"But where should we begin?" asked several students when we returned to Room 405. The excitement in the hallway cafeteria yielded to fears of not knowing how to get the job done and potentially not reaching the ultimate goal. My ideas about how to proceed remained vague, and instead of giving explicit directions, I was interested in my students' thoughts. This concept of asking students is encouraged in teacher preparation programs. Usually it is under the assumption that teachers manipulate the situation so students feel as though they are in control, when in reality the teacher planned the process and prescribed the outcome. In our case, I really didn't know what would become of our ideas but was willing to risk the potential outcomes, even failures, so the experience could have genuine consequences—both good and bad—and the fight could be authentic.

The class needed a plan of attack, one that would allow the students to select areas of interest to them individually, while at the same time staying organized. From my educational training, I had learned it was often customary to cover the curriculum for the entire classroom without direct attention to adjusting learning opportunities for the highest achievers or struggling students. "Don't be too challenging or too easy" and "Teach to the middle group of learners" were words of wisdom repeatedly proclaimed during my teacher preparation. Feeling this typical approach was grossly inadequate, I sought to teach against it. As I brooded over my questioning, I decided my students should choose their own areas of interest and subsequently share their findings with the class as they progressed. Not having a model progressive educator in the school,

I found myself reading about teachers and curriculum theorizers who had explored similar approaches in developing curricula adapted to each student's needs.

The class agreed that the first step included researching the history of Carr Community Academy and investigating the potential for getting a new school built. All the students knew a school had been promised by the Chicago Public Schools six years earlier (Chicago Public Schools, 1999; Weissman, 1996). Looking hard enough through the foggy bulletproof windows, or peering through the only glass window, which was cracked and pocked with a bullet hole, the students could see a sign on an adjacent fenced-off property proclaiming the site of the "Future Carr Elementary." If that was not disconcerting enough, the architectural plans depicting the new school design were displayed in the lobby of our dilapidated building. Years earlier the school faculty had picked out everything for the new building from paint to tiles, and even window treatments, yet no action had been taken. The promises by the board of education and city of Chicago were empty ones.

Discussing Multiple Approaches

During our brainstorming session, the students began to create rough ideas of direction. In my journal I wrote that they got really passionate, almost out of control, but were great about generating ideas, so part of me wanted them to be as wild and creative as they wanted. In the midst of their intense discussion, they proposed ways to take action. From their dialogue, main ideas emerged: "people we can talk to," "getting in newspapers and magazines," and "putting pressure on people."

Previously in class discussion, or problem-solving in general, students rarely considered multiple approaches. This project, however, presented something genuine, and the students understood the need to approach the task from many angles. They weren't satisfied with just one avenue. Acknowledging the complexity of the problem, the students determined that several prongs were necessary for their effort to be worthwhile.

Like typical fifth graders, once a good idea was raised, several students wanted to take instantaneous action rather than continuing the brainstorming process. When the principal was selected as a potential interviewee, several students wanted to leave immediately because, as Demetrius commented, "He can mos def help us!" Although each new idea brought excitement, the students needed redirection to maintain focus and increase options. Luckily, as I wrote in my journal, "Everyone agreed that planning was essential rather than acting on impulse."

Was my intervention steering the curriculum too much? Was it right for me to try convincing students to stay on task to develop the action plan more fully? Despite my apprehension, I understood that I did not want them to miss out on the discussion or leave without hearing everyone's valuable input.

The list generated of people we could talk to was long and thorough, including names of potential decision makers that I would have left off my list. The list included members of the school administration, leaders in area politics, the board of education, and corporate friends of the school. It was gratifying that students listened to the suggestions of the people already interviewed—Mr. Wurtzman and Reverend Tinter—and that other key informants were included who might help provide information and influence for the campaign. Our work was certainly cut out for us.

The students focused next on newspapers and magazines they believed could help get the word out about their need for a new school. They noted that the *Chicago Tribune* and *Chicago Sun-Times* were the big city papers. As one student exclaimed, "It be cool to have our mugs in the real papers." Kamala also mentioned that his grandma was always reading a paper that "was for Chicago Black folk called the *Defender*." He thought, "We'd have good chances of them bein' interested in us." The students also latched onto the possibility of getting the Chicago television stations to cover their story.

Students had the foresight to include "ways to put pressure" as a means of achieving their goal. In touch with techniques for active participation in our democracy, they were familiar with the lingo and ways to get engaged, yet they had never been activists before. Their list included: surveying kids and teachers, circulating a petition, interviewing powerful people in the community, writing letters to legislators, holding a press conference, and developing a documentary video. If we were able to accomplish these things, not only was the classroom curriculum going to be driven by the students' interests, it was going to be vibrant for all of us. Each technique could not happen in a single class period or over a simple curriculum unit. The ideas were going to take research, investigation, planning, and dedication to be accomplished. Whereas I was more than willing to support them in these efforts, I was skeptical regarding their commitment to following through with their plan.

My uncertainty about potentially pursuing an uncertain path was nerve-racking, yet premature. If the curriculum followed the students' suggestions, we would have to forgo the prescriptive, teacher-proof lessons, but the state standards would still need to be addressed in an indirect manner, rather than artificially front-loading them into daily activities. This was uncharted territory—beyond my experience—and certainly beyond the scope of Project Citizen. But this was exactly what I hoped to foster, and there was no way I was going to hinder its progress.

Researching and Organizing Information

Our discussion led to ways of gathering information. The students offered many suggestions, including researching in newspapers, looking on the Internet, continuing to interview, and inviting guests to the school to help with our plans. Once the students saw research as a way to further their cause, they began asking specific questions they wanted answered and requested a way to organize all the information.

During January, I had attended a workshop presented by the literacy expert credited with developing the K-W-L chart. The K-W-L is an instructional reading strategy that helps guide students through text. When teachers use the K-W-L chart in their classrooms, they elicit what students "know" about a topic; students then have the opportunity to ask questions about what they "want to know," followed with discussion and documentation about what they "learned" after the reading (Ogle, 1986). At this session, a different version of the K-W-L chart, called an I-chart or inquiry-chart, was presented (Hoffman, 1992). Using the I-chart as a means to guide student research, students can present findings through a planned framework for inquiring about important questions by applying what they already know to what they discover through supplemental sources.

Several weeks after attending the workshop, back in the classroom, I presented a blank I-chart, spanning the entire chalkboard. The students were neither supportive nor enthusiastic. It looked daunting and overwhelming.

"That color paper is ugly!" yelled out Terrance.

"You crazy! We ain't filling all that out!" shouted another.

Initially frustrated by the ridicule and after losing my temper, I regained composure. After all, it was the students who wanted something to organize the information they had found. Redirecting several students with a somewhat impatient, "That is not appropriate in my classroom," I explained, "Much of the questions and information for the chart have already been discovered." Eventually we came up with guiding questions to help better understand the history, decision making, gentrification, and other reasons for the lack of a new school. Along one axis, we had a column dedicated to what we already knew, and the rest of the chart was left blank for what we anticipated learning from our sources.

Data sources from the students' Internet searches were the starting point. They were so accustomed to bookmarking their favorites that it was easy to aggregate the material. The students had found pertinent newspaper and magazine articles, television broadcasts, Board of Education documents, and Web sites with large amounts of data to help us gain insight.

There was so much information gathered that I could not dedicate enough time to reading everything before the students got to the documents. In small groups, they tackled the articles. This was a first glimpse of the dedication and reading perseverance my students were going to exhibit during the project, as most of the articles were written well above their (supposed) reading level.

As the time flew by during their reading and subsequent research findings, the students shouted out some of the most important facts and implications. They were no longer resistant to the chart that continuously filled up with additional sources and facts through the ongoing discovery. The use of this organizational tool not only allowed the students to get the resources quickly, it also allowed them to find articles they were most comfortable with based on their ability to understand the text. Since there were many sources at varying difficulty levels, I purposefully tried to meet individual needs when passing out the articles. Interestingly, the students sought out articles and information they were familiar with from their own searches regardless of complexity.

During the activity, pedagogical questions arose. Was this reading method appropriate, and how could I monitor all the students in the class simultaneously? Should students go through articles together, or should they try to find the best method for reading difficult material on their own? They appreciated the autonomy in reading the articles and were eager to get the data onto the I-chart; however, their findings were riddled with errors. I struggled with allowing them to champion what they believed was accurate while still maintaining their enthusiasm.

Before I could intervene, the students came up with a way to solve the problem. A couple of the stronger readers also noticed the problem and took it upon themselves to develop a screening process. The due diligence and self-regulation provided a means for the I-chart to take shape, develop as a resource, and remain a fixture for the remainder of the year.

As the research provided a foundation toward achieving their ambitious goal, the students continued brainstorming ways to influence change. They wanted to petition the community to ask for help and inform citizens of the dire situation at Carr. While touting civil disobedience through a school boycott or strike, they vowed to continue writing letters and photographing. They also believed that creating a video documentary and getting in the newspapers could help the cause. Several suggested fund-raisers like car washes or selling candy as potential ideas, while others were quick to criticize the idea because it would simply "be too many candy bars to make 18 million for a new school!" as one said.

As the ideas continued, the students were obviously picking and choosing their main areas of interest. I heard one say, "My mama ain't gonna let me go round my street to get signatures—its too dangerous in d'hood," while others were abuzz about the "coolness of makin' a video." As students called out, I heard someone say, "We needin' them pizza things." Not understanding, I let it pass so I could hear others' ideas, but he persisted.

"We need to have them pizza things, Mr. Schultz!" exclaimed Terrance. I turned toward the small boy. His eye contact and serious expression forced me to listen.

"Terrance, what are you talking about?" I responded as respectfully as I could amidst the chaos of other suggestions being shouted out.

"Come on, y'know, them those things that are in the newspapers all the time, y'know, them circle things with different colors."

As I looked quizzically at Terrance, still not understanding what he was talking about, Reggie blurted out, "You mean pie charts?"

Curious about whether Terrance or any of his classmates knew why they might be helpful, I asked, "Why would we want to have pie charts?"

Terrance explained we needed to have them, "'Cause they important."

The dialogue continued as I kept prompting for more information.

"The newspapers use them for proving things. We know they important and they can help us get a new school so we's got to have 'em," he said. And with that, he satisfied the others and me. Them pizza things got added to our action plan.

"We can make those charts when we do the surveys," Reggie added.

Once the students understood that the project direction was in their control, the development of tangible action-oriented steps came alive. Quickly realizing that organization was key to making the dream of a new school a reality, the students put in extra time to accomplish the task. Dyneisha and Malik volunteered to stay after school to put together a

PowerPoint presentation so the action plan would be clear for work the next day. As the two sat over the computer arguing over placement, style, and colors, they remained focused on developing an easy-to-read diagram that incorporated the ideas generated by the class.

Launching an Action Plan

So much was happening, and so fast! The weekend gave me time to reflect. Comments in a journal entry from the second week of February revealed my astonishment about how the project was taking over the curriculum. In the span of just days, the students wrote their first journal entries, interviewed the LSC president, and formulated an action plan. I had mixed emotions. Although ecstatic about the potential, I was concerned about how everything I was supposed to teach would get covered in the

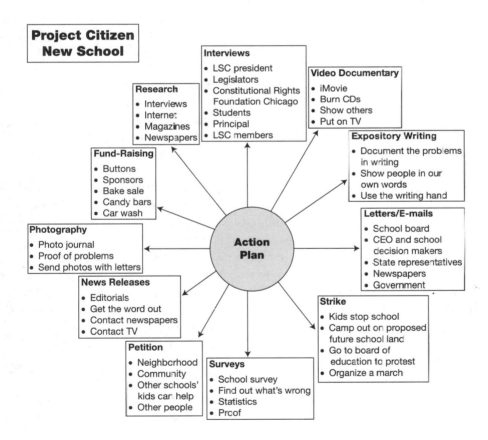

school day. Every period of every day was becoming part of the student-directed project.

This had become a real, integrated, and authentic curriculum that came from the students. It was beginning to connect subject matters and was fulfilling their needs and desires. The process was what I had imagined, but it was frightening, too. I was concerned about setting the students up for failure. They were taking on the infamous city government of Chicago—certainly no simple feat! Although I wanted to have the students create everything, I felt a responsibility to help organize the project so they would be able to reach their objectives. But how was I going to be able to control and predict the outcomes, while also ensuring they were learning all the required material, when I didn't know where the project would lead us?

I spent the following weekend devising an approach using the students' ideas. Different groups would be dedicated to each part of the action plan. The class was divided into interview, survey, petition, video documentary, editorial, and pamphlet/letter-writing clusters based on their interests. I wrestled with how so many different focuses could be managed all at once. Was there a way to teach minilessons on each segment of the plan so everyone could learn everything, or should we really divide, delegate, and conquer the various action plan items separately without making sure each student was able to take away the same learning? I wanted to keep up the momentum and illustrate that it was possible for kids to make change if they were organized and persistent. Showing examples of other kids' efforts with social action projects was one method of helping the students realize this idea (see Lewis, Espeland, & Pernu, 1998).

Group formation began based on the students' interests. My goal was to use a classroom volunteer as a guide to work with what I considered the easiest group of students. There was a group of retired businesspeople who had been volunteering regularly at Carr. One gentleman in particular had taken a liking to several students in Room 405 and dropped by a couple of times a month. I thought that this way everyone could achieve success. He worked with Reggie, Shaniqua, Jaris, and Dyneisha on developing the survey. Their goal would be to eventually analyze data from a student-centered survey so they could use it as evidence to get people "to support us," just as Terrance and Reggie had discussed in terms of "them pizza things."

The rest of the children went into the hallway with me. My intention was to find a way to approach the multiple groups with interests in different parts of the plan. Even though I could not guide pamphlet-makers, petitioners, and video documentarians all at once, I decided to take this large group into the technology lab myself as I attempted to harness their enthusiasm. I suspected getting immediate input rather than letting them go in different directions without guidance would be the best way to proceed. In my journal, I wrote that I was a bit tentative about changing course, since students had just been allowed to self-select into groups. This was not a bad thing—everyone would participate in everything to some degree—but was I inhibiting their motivation and empowerment by pushing them in the same direction? I convinced them, and more importantly myself, that this large group would initially focus on one part of the action plan and then proceed to the other parts.

We decided collectively to begin with petitions. While I was explaining the essence of petitioning, Malik interrupted me, explaining to his peers that "a petition could help us raise awareness and get support for d'cause." Malik was aware of community members seeking a referendum to stop demolition of Cabrini buildings, and his interjection was extremely relevant.

With this context provided by Malik, students decided that each kid could get a certain number of signatures. As they shared their prior knowledge through storytelling about how they'd seen people with clipboards getting signatures to prevent the Reds (tenement buildings) being torn down, I encouraged them to write a pitch requesting supporters' signatures. My amazement with how focused the group was during the talk about petitioning and how quickly a catchphrase was coined to get others involved was noted in my journal. Their call for a new building was explicit and compelling:

> PLEASE HELP CARR ACADEMY STUDENTS!!!
> There are a lot of problems with William D. Carr Community Academy. We think it needs replacement. Please sign your name if you agree that we need a new school.

Following the session, I outlined in my journal connections between subjects: "As the petition was created, the civics lesson transitioned into a math problem. It seemed natural to connect the subjects this way. As I questioned students about how many signatures were necessary, they deliberated about what amount would help the cause." After one boy suggested 300, another reminded him there were more people than that in the school alone. Demetrius stepped up to take charge. Leading a discussion of his peers, he went to the chalkboard to begin scribbling down various math equations based on several proposed scenarios. As he instructed the class, Demetrius announced to his attentive peers what he believed was the best solution: "If there are 16 students and everyone got 125 signatures, there would be 2000 signatures. That should definitely convince the decision makers we need a whole new school!"

Applying math skills to the project, Demetrius not only listened to his classmates' ideas but now had taken on a leadership role. Acting as the "petition manager," Demetrius asserted control rather than having me assign it. Using his skills, know-how, and charisma, Demetrius captured his peers' attention and delivered an excellent math lesson.

Returning to the classroom, the petitioners were eager to share their ideas. Demetrius gladly explained the petition, its inherent math and civics components, and his expectations of everyone. Rather than challenging his stern demands as they most certainly would have done to mine, the students respectfully agreed, applauding his presentation.

The survey group then had the opportunity to present their results. Reggie explained that he had already created questions in his journal, and the rest of the group went along with his ideas. Interestingly, in the survey cohort, leadership roles also emerged among the students. I was proud of Reggie for sharing his efforts, especially since he had a tendency to be selfish with his ideas and work. Although initially impressed with the presentation, when I glanced at the survey coming off the printer, I realized there was a major flaw in its design.

Reggie and his classmates had certainly created a survey, but it asked only open-ended questions! Although I was frustrated that the volunteer had not guided the group in the manner I might have, it would prove to be a learning opportunity for everyone. As the survey crew shared their work with the class, they were on edge, believing that by the day's end they would have some results. Before I had the opportunity to raise my concern about the inadequate survey, Dyneisha and Shaniqua had collected a stack from the printer and asked permission to take them to the fourth graders. Not wanting to impede their enthusiasm, I granted permission.

The two girls went down to a fourth-grade classroom with the five-question assessment. According to input from the fourth-grade teacher, the girls did not give direction to their younger peers but insisted the students fill out the survey immediately. Each younger student willingly completed it, and the girls hastily returned to Room 405.

As they began sharing the results aloud, Tavon questioned how the results were going "to show all them answers on them charts." Stumped by the query, the girls looked to Reggie, the question developer, but he, too, had no answers. This had the potential to be a perfect learning experience. The students could discover what it took to develop a survey to make the pie charts, but they would have to learn by what I called "falling forward."

I was pleased when Tavon pointed out the misstep of having open-ended questions. The room fell silent for what seemed like minutes until Reggie realized, "If we had multiple-choice answers to each question, we would be able to make pie charts from these results." The class had collided with an obstacle, but with their problem-solving skills developing, they were willing and able to overcome the barrier. Collectively, they found the problem, put their heads together, and solved it!

This was a great point of reflection for me as a teacher. If I had been in the room at the time when the survey was created, I would have certainly intervened, never allowing them to go in the "wrong direction." I would have challenged them to "think harder," leading them to believe there was a better approach for developing a survey. Instead, they took the initiative themselves; they learned they could go about the process differently to yield the desired results. In this case, rather than failing, they fell forward and were able to figure it out on their own. This was far more valuable than any scripted process I could have taught for developing a survey.

Reggie shared that he was not stumped by the predicament. He went back to the computer and modified the original work. The rest of his survey group was not as enthusiastic. They felt the work had already been done. Regardless of their frustration, Reggie was willing to re-create the questionnaire—even willing at that moment to perhaps take on an unfair share of work—so the newly created survey would generate meaningful data and could be used to produce the envisioned pie charts. With the inclination to develop closed-ended, multiple-choice questions, they were making progress. Although I wanted to see an equitable distribution of the workload among students, I understood some students' aggravation with the situation. I realized that the challenge of this kind of problem solving meant that some students were going to step up while others were not as engaged. I wondered if my lack of insistence for continuous classwide participation provided a richer experience for some students more than others.

The dynamics of these events were particularly interesting. The students weren't in agreement, but the opportunity presented itself for several to take on different responsibilities. Assuming atypical roles, students were recognized for their insight, creativity, and leadership. Their classmates now had reasons beyond social status to look up to their peers. Numerous students began getting deserved respect for their efforts. Negativity subsided as everyone worked toward a greater good, putting differences and friendships aside, to further the cause.

3

Getting the Word Out: Sharing Authority in Room 405

YOU WOULDN'T LET YOUR KIDS COME TO A SCHOOL THAT IS FALLING APART

"We need to take this to the street," called out Dyneisha.

By mid-February, the students had shown they were committed. The classroom talk clearly demonstrated they believed in working for the shared cause. And Dyneisha was right, but before we could start gathering signatures and presenting their cause, an informational packet needed to be put together. Without input from me, the kids decided what to include in their promotional materials. During a classroom forum, students listened, made suggestions, and eventually decided what they believed would make the packet complete. The initial draft included the laundry list of everything wrong with the community, the graphic organizer of all the school's problems, each student's expository text, and Demetrius's photo journal, since it "would let everyone see the problems for themselves," as Tavon indicated. Jaris suggested the petition be put up front, since "it was the most important part."

With piles of copies sitting on a classroom table, the students decided the folders ought to be red so they would attract attention. Leaving Reggie and Jaris in charge, I stepped out of the room to meet with a parent. When I got back, I was presented with a classic situation. The boys had hurriedly assembled all the information. In their haste, they had punched holes on the wrong side of each document. Rather than keeping it professional, the boys simply rotated the documents and repunched them, latching the papers into the folder prongs. The extra holes were keen reminders of the project ambassadors—a bunch of fifth graders! Although I contemplated intervening to suggest redoing the packets with only a single set of hole punches, I chose not to interfere since they did not see it as problematic and were adamant about swiftly finishing the folders.

Now that the information packets were taking shape, the surveys were even more essential. I felt that it was appropriate to accompany the surveyors to each classroom to ensure a proper representation. We returned to the class that had previously been surveyed with the open-ended questionnaires. Even though we rehearsed what to say, when we arrived at the third-floor room, the kids froze. I made a mental note to develop a written script for students.

Once the surveying team returned to our classroom, their demeanors changed: "They were the wildest I had ever seen them. They were so excited and passionate to share their experience with the entire class," I wrote in my journal. It was incongruous to me after witnessing their flustered delivery just minutes earlier. Many other teachers would have seen this class as out of control. Although I wanted and supported the students' fervor, didn't I need to do a better job managing and containing their excitement? It was not easy to encourage them to get excited while controlling their typical age-related behaviors. Was it going to be possible to go through all their ideas and have them be respectful at the same time?

There were other classrooms to visit for data collection. As we went around the school, the kids barged in without explaining their interruption. What happened to our written scripts? Although there were remarkable scenes, especially watching fifth graders work with the pre-K kids, helping them to fill out the survey (guiding them to the answers they wanted), I would have been annoyed if another group acted in the manner my students handled themselves. The unruly behavior forced me to revisit the approach. I reflected in my journal that it is empowering to go room to room but that the students needed to be more courteous. As a result of how I was interpreting their behavior, I decided that the survey would be distributed to teachers and they could return them to my mailbox to contain the project. Further, I noted that, although cute, it was a bit disconcerting to have the fifth graders coercing their younger peers.

This decision was tough. I encouraged students to steer the project, but I also had to find an appropriate method for their interacting with others. After all, it was my role to enforce acceptable school behavior. Although aiming to have students do everything, I quickly realized that this utopian ideal wasn't possible; they couldn't even handle the autonomy of going to another room! Additionally, it was a disappointment that collecting the answers to the survey was going to take time.

Not even a week after the surveys were distributed to the teachers' mailboxes, we received more responses than I ever anticipated getting. Once the surveys were in hand, I could have taken the data to crunch the numbers. But wouldn't the entire process lose its integrity and its student ownership if I did it? Hadn't I already intervened enough regarding the survey delivery?

What sense would it make to have the students define the questions, collect the data, and then have me make the charts? If this was to be theirs, there needed to be a kid-friendly, aptitude-appropriate way to accomplish this. Fortunately, a component of the Collaboratory was a survey tool. The students were familiar with this resource from earlier work but had not designed anything on it themselves. With the help of a couple of fifth graders from the survey team, the students and I designed the online tool together.

Data entry took place the next morning. The survey team divided the completed forms among the class. After the initial instructions, they informed their peers to repeat the process until all surveys were entered. By teaching each other, the students showed how well they understood the process and the subject at hand.

In the meantime, other orders of business needed attention. The students eagerly prepared for a visit by an acquaintance of the principal, Melvin Mayfield, who had grown up in the Cabrini Green neighborhood and was now a successful businessman. Upon his arrival, the students commented how "slick he looked" and perhaps "he can buy us a new school heself."

Mayfield spoke to the students for about an hour, but he was different from earlier visitors to our classroom. It was evident that Mayfield established himself as a positive role model. Discussing various business connections to stress how important it was to build relationships, he wowed the fifth graders. After enthusiastically going around the room to find out what each wanted to be when he or she grew up, he challenged them with backup ideas to their dreams of becoming football players or musicians. As the interview continued, he explained the frustrations he faced in school and talked about how being labeled learning-disabled had affected him throughout his tenure in Cabrini Green elementary classrooms. They intently listened, especially in regard to his comments about being persistent and always reaching for something better.

The students patiently waited to have the man in front with his "wingtips and style-ly pressed suit" give them the attention they sought. I listened as he offered to present the problems at Carr to some businesspeople and ask them for donations to help fund their cause. At the moment, the lofty goal of getting a new building seemed like a reality to many of the students in Room 405. "A real connection to some Black folk," as one student said, may have gotten them the spotlight they needed.

As the students went to gym, I knew there would be much to reflect on about his visit. Although the kids were totally into the idea, I was skeptical, since the issue was certainly bigger than one person with good connections. Although it was great to have a responsible, professional role model originally from their community, it seemed too good to be true, and I was afraid the promises might not be realized.

Two days after Mayfield's visit, I saw the Local School Council president in the school office. I gave him an update on the events that had been occurring. Tinter said he felt this whole thing was getting really good. Since the project was gaining momentum, he expressed interest in sending out a press release. He wanted the students to draft a letter that he would pick up two days later!

I really believed the encouragement the LSC president gave the students and me was wonderful. A powerful community member articulated his support for my efforts as a teacher, but truth be told, I had concerns that the curriculum might be taken away from the students if I followed through with his requests. His eagerness for big-time publicity without understanding the theoretical underpinnings of the classroom made my reservations more pronounced.

The situation's complexity tested my pedagogical integrity. In some ways this could become a self-serving situation for classroom outsiders, rather than a learning opportunity for the students. It was obviously in his interest to get publicity for the issues of the school, and the class could benefit from it. He had significant connections that I simply did not have. While I believe he genuinely had students in mind, and undoubtedly had good intentions, this presented a dilemma that I did not know how to handle.

At home that night, I was both excited and confused. I needed to make a decision that could affect the way the project turned out. I felt uncomfortable not overseeing the project, but I had thought the struggle would be with students rather than a request made by the LSC president.

Having someone else use their ideas could lead to exploitation of the students, and they might miss out on learning opportunities if someone else made the decisions. As the teacher, I was now forced to determine the project parameters. I needed to find a way to serve the best interests of students while simultaneously making certain the desires of the supportive LSC president were met, too. If the backing was to continue, I would have to satisfy Tinter as well; I just wondered if the kids were going to get lost in the shuffle.

The next day, I detailed Tinter's request to the students. Given the enthusiastic student response to the LSC president's appeal, I described how their expository writing could be transformed into a persuasive statement. The students combined their individual work to create a powerful letter that would be sent to the school board, city officials, newspaper and television reporters, and concerned citizens. In the letter, students documented the school's tremendous problems that were "not fixable." Strategically, they invited the reader "to see our school for yourself." As they stated, "We do not think you would let your kids come to a school that is falling apart." With their provocative invitation, the students laid a strong foundation for the social action curriculum project to take off.

Although the letter was longer than necessary, the students worked collectively, offering the best work from their own essays. As we read it aloud, the students put various sections together as they vividly described the shameful state of the school. As students chose some parts and tweaked others, their words took shape as I facilitated best practices of developing a persuasive statement. In the end, as a class, they figured out how to transform their expository text into a strong, coherent, and convincing letter. This letter would become an important milestone in their quest for a new school.

Since there had been such pressure by Reverend Tinter to get the letter out quickly, I took the students' compilation home that night. Although they had manipulated all of their texts into one document, I felt it still needed a little finesse to make it presentable to Tinter and other readers. Struggling again with what was appropriate in this situation, I felt I had moral obligations to my students and myself in regard to using their original craft. As I put finishing touches on the letter, I was careful to change very little, believing it was essential to leave it in the students' voice. Once it was proofread, I felt comfortable with my decision and felt that any changes made were subtle enough that it was still wholeheartedly theirs.

February 20, 2004
To Whom It May Concern:
We are writing to tell you about exciting work our fifth-grade class is doing called Project Citizen. This project is sponsored by the Constitutional Rights Foundation of Chicago. It teaches us about how the government works and how we can affect public policy change even as fifth graders. Our class has looked at all the problems that affect our community and have unanimously decided to focus our attention on the policy of building new schools in the City of Chicago. We have created an action plan that includes researching, petitioning, surveying, writing, photography and also interviewing and writing letters to people we think can help us fix the policy. We think and hope you would be interested in hearing about all the problems that our school in Cabrini Green is faced with everyday.
Our school building, William D. Carr Academy, has big problems. There are too many problems to mention in this letter, but we want to tell you about some of the most important ones. These main problems are what we think are important issues: the restrooms, temperature in our building, the windows and the lack of a lunchroom, a gym and a stage. We need a new school because of these problems. It is really important for our learning so we can be great when we grow up.
The restrooms are filthy and dirty. There are spitballs all over the place. They do not get cleaned up properly. It is also really smelly in the bathrooms. Also, we do not have soap or paper towels or garbage cans. We do not have doors on the stall and have no privacy. The sinks have bugs in them and water is everywhere. As an example of how bad they are, sinks move and water leaks on the floor. The hot water

faucets have cold water. Kids don't like using the bathrooms since they are so gross and falling apart.

In fact at Carr the temperatures in the classrooms are broken. The heat is not turned on. It is really cold in the classrooms. As another example we have to put on our coats during class because it is so cold. They cannot fix it because the pipes are broken. It is uncomfortable and hard to learn. Our hands are cold and we cannot write. This needs to be changed!

As another example the windows are cracked. It is cold in our class because the windows are cracked. The windows are not efficient enough. There are bullet holes in the windows and there is tape on them. We cannot see through the windows and it is dark in the classrooms. We can hardly see what we are doing because it is so dark. This is not a good place to learn.

Another reason we need a new building is that we don't have a lunchroom. We eat in a hallway! The classes by the lunchroom are always getting distracted because of the lunchroom in the hall. That is why we need a new lunchroom so the classes will not be getting distracted. Another bad thing about our lunchroom is we don't get to decide what we want in lunch. Also, we want vending machines so we can eat a little snack to give us energy so we can learn better. Our school really needs a new lunchroom because the lunchroom lady shouldn't have to tell students to be quiet. The teachers by the lunchroom shouldn't have to close their doors to teach.

Another example of the problem is the gym is not connected to our school. Whenever it's bad weather outside we have to walk through the snow. In fact, it is not even our gym. We borrow a gym from Seward Park across the street. It is dangerous crossing the street and we shouldn't have to cross the street during school. This takes up our gym period. When we have basketball practice we get locked out because Seward Park is not open. If we had our own gym in our school we wouldn't get locked out or be faced with the weather. When we walk to the gym its ice on the ground. One day a little kid got hurt from falling on the ice.

Finally, we also do not have an auditorium or stage at Carr. This is a problem because when we have assemblies, people heads are in the way because we have to have the assemblies in a hallway. There is no seating and it is difficult to see. There are never enough seats for

everybody and people have to stand. As an example, we had the
Harlem Globetrotters come to our school. We couldn't see anything. If
are school had a stage we would be happy because we would have a
better chance to watch the show.

We would like to invite you to see our school for yourself. We do
not think that you would let your kids come to a school that is falling
apart. Since the windows, the gym, the temperature, the lunchroom,
stage, and restrooms are not right we should get a whole new school
building. The problems are not fixable and would cost too much to fix.
Carr Academy needs a new school building and the current policy has
promised us one but it has not been built.

There are many reasons why we need a new school and we think
you would agree. A new school would be a better school and we believe
we will get a better education. We have the support of our teacher and
of the administration of the school for this project. We look forward to
hearing from you and thank you in advance for your time and interest.

Respectfully yours,
The Fifth Graders in Room 405
William D. Carr Community Academy

WHEN ARE WE GOING TO DO WORK?

The students' efforts had gathered significant momentum. Indeed, as one
student put it, "We learned petitioning is an important way to get support
because everyone we show our materials to wants to support us." Besides,
who could argue with children when their documentation exposed specific, negligent actions by the city of Chicago and the board of education?

The students' interest in going into the community to garner support
was apparent the first weekend of petition gathering. Even students who
had difficulty in written work evolved into excellent oral communicators,
and almost every student returned from the weekend with multiple pages
of signatures supporting the "new school for Carr."

Darnell, who usually found it difficult to express himself on paper,
flourished with the opportunity to vocalize his ideas. Following his first
weekend petitioning, he dictated a journal entry. He stated, "I feel successful with the petitions because it was fun and it made me feel like I am great
'cause I got the most signatures in the class . . . . People agreed that Carr
needs a new school. I like it when people agree with me."

Darnell's articulation in his journaling shows that he was able to find his comfort zone. He realized he was recognized in his classroom as the best, something he had never before felt among his peers. Darnell now had a reason to excel, and it came from his experience petitioning.

Similarly, Shaniqua said, "It's a fun activity for us to do. If we want a school we have to work as hard as we can . . . we also got help learning how to be brave . . . and telling others what we are working on." The petitioning forced the students to present tangible evidence to a wide audience, summarize their goals, and address why they were taking action. It allowed them to ask others for help in accomplishing their goals while they acted as spokespeople for the desired changes.

As each part of the action plan took on a life of its own, the students assigned different class members to each plan area. Students self-selected roles, and the class nominated individuals to be team leaders. It was impressive that the students delegated responsibilities and made certain to put someone in charge. Darnell, for example, became the co-manager of the petitions because of his newfound success.

Working as a team, they looked to their peers for direction, readily listening to their classmates when given instructions or goals for each part of the plan. Had I been designating tasks, they might not have been so enthusiastic or attentive. As it was, the students were generating the ideas, and consensus was being reached on almost every decision through the democratic process, as these fifth graders and I became totally absorbed in their project.

"Mr. Schultz, when are we going to start doing work?" queried Artell as he arranged his completed petition sheets in the front of his folder. Initially puzzled by his question, I realized he was referring to the usual routine of worksheets, memorization, and rote learning. He had been "working" harder and more purposefully than before the start of this project, but due to the manner in which American schools condition students, he did not feel he was really completing schoolwork. His comment was a startling revelation of the educational methods that are actually used in most schools today. The education-with-a-purpose, learning-by-doing mantra commonplace in Room 405 was having a great impact on these students.

The Girls Won! Owning and Making Sense of Their Data

Our goal was to use the data to create pie charts and graphs, but how? Instead of direct instruction, I encouraged the children to determine how to create pie charts and graphs on their own.

The class divided into several small groups. Although I could easily have created charts for students to interpret, this was not the approach I wanted to take. Certainly the interpretation could have been a very rewarding experience, but I realized the students should have the opportunity to make sense of data. Each step could, should, and would become a learning experience.

After the groups shared their ideas on how to get the data into charts and graphs, I suggested using the Collaboratory to organize our data and view the results. I gave direction and advice, but the students took over the direction of the evaluation. It would become a new experience for everyone, including me. The outputs from the Collaboratory would have a kid-friendly interface, and it would provide them with additional information to influence others.

The next morning, an hour before they needed to be in the building, several students were awaiting my arrival. This had become standard, as the kids enjoyed working through their ideas and sorting through the various issues early in the morning, a marked contrast to the previous school year, when it had been a struggle to have my students even arrive on time. With an open-door policy, they felt safe and comfortable in the classroom. These early birds organized the information for the rest of the class and waited for the others to arrive so we could head to the computer lab and enter our data.

After almost two hours of data entry, the students did not need to be told to look at their results. They understood the derived information without instruction. They owned the data and quickly interpreted and shared the outcomes with one another, jumping between the pie charts and bar graphs on their monitors.

As everyone sorted through "them pizza-things-pie-charts," in exasperation Hennessy shouted out, "Man, the girls won!"

The girls won? What was he talking about? Calling me to his computer, and with several students craning their necks to peer over his shoulder, he pointed to the results showing that the girls had a larger portion of the pie than the boys. He concluded, based on this observation, "The girls won."

"Since more girls responded to our survey than boys, the girls simply had a bigger portion of the pie; it was not a win-or-lose situation," I explained.

Hennessy was confused by my explanation. But as others gathered around him, there was an opportunity to make an addition to their vocabulary. "When there is the most of something in your results, we call that the mode."

Over the next 15 minutes, it was apparent through my questions that they were making additional discoveries, but I was unsure whether they understood the new terminology.

Suddenly, to my surprise, Malik called out, "Mr. Schultz, Mr. Schultz! The mode for the problems with d'school is d'bootleg lunchroom. People think where we eat is the biggest problem." With Malik's comment—a student with one of the lowest aptitudes according to standardized test scores—it was obvious that the students understood their data.

This was one of those great learning moments for me as the teacher. According to the state learning standards, this sort of data interpretation was not necessarily expected of students in the fifth grade. These students were readily doing data analysis because the information belonged to them! Rather than using a didactic approach to teaching about data analysis, this guided method of teaching through hands-on experience provided a better way for the students to understand the material.

From determining what questions to ask to actually making sense of the graphs, these students were applying their real-life interpretation to data analysis. This material had real substance and value, and it was going to ultimately help with their cause. It was remarkable to hear classroom talk about averages, means, modes, and computing percentages for each question. Refreshingly, we were not open to Chapter 12 in our math book. There were no words to memorize. Rather, they were experientially demonstrating an understanding from what they had collected.

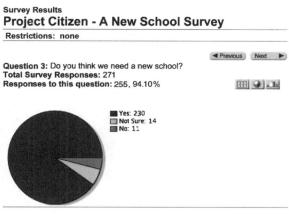

A page from a student's information packet originally created using tools from the Collaboratory Project.

One boy clearly articulated the purpose: "We now have more evidence to share with people who might sign our petition." The students eagerly printed copies to be added to their information packets to prove to people the existence of all the problems with the school.

Becoming More Experienced at Making Connections

With the remaining data from the petitions forthcoming, the students continued to get responses from their letter campaign. Not only did encouragement and praise come their way, they also received donations to help with the cause. One letter contained postage stamps, telling the class "to keep the letter writing coming" and "hopes this would help with some of the costs." Other letters had personal checks, and some even contained cash. A special account was set up with the school's business manager, and the students monitored its use. Astonished by the generosity of strangers, Shaniqua remarked, "This is so great! People are sending us money that don't even know us." As the correspondence continued, the students developed relationships with some of the concerned citizens.

One such advocate was William Ayers, a professor of mine at the University of Illinois at Chicago. Ayers's reputation for championing social justice education, his experiences as an activist and teacher in various capacities, and his prolific writing about these topics made him an excellent ally. After receiving their letter, Ayers visited the class to discuss ways they could continue with their action plan. As he encouraged them to rally others to their cause, many of his suggestions were met with students showing him how they had already begun in that direction. Although he repeated "many of their ideas," as Shaniqua said, the students were impressed with him. Terrance commented, "He remembered all of our names just by meeting us once!" Others, like Hennessy, thought it was a great thing to have him, since "he is your teacher and you are our teacher all in the same room." Ayers encouraged the students to ask others to write letters on their behalf, explaining that it might help persuade more people to listen to their goals. Upon his departure, he promised to write a letter—excerpted below—to Chicago's decision makers describing what he had witnessed in the classroom. Ayers wrote:

> I met recently with a bright, energetic group of fifth-grade students at Carr Academy. . . . They have been working for months on a thoughtful and creative social studies project of immediate relevance and

urgency to them: investigating the conditions of their building. They have conducted surveys, dug into history, compared the physical plant at Carr with other school facilities, and they are beginning an advocacy campaign, circulating petitions, contacting the media and concerned citizens. They are exploring all kinds of ways to engage the public. . . .

As I was leaving class, one of their vocal members asked me if I thought powerful people would listen to "just a group of fifth-graders." I told her there was only one way to find out: speak-up, write letters, invite them to meet with you and then see who rises to the moment. I urge you to respond to them. . . . You will find a propulsive and engaging group of young citizens worthy of your deepest concern and your best effort.

The students embraced Ayers's advice and continued on their quest.

"Techniques for Participation"

Encouraging the students to be active change agents, I introduced them to a book entitled *Civics for Democracy: A Journey for Teachers and Students* (Isaac, 1992). I thought the section "Techniques for Participation" would give the students momentum that would allow them to expand their efforts and offer more ways to get others "to rise to the moment," as Ayers had suggested.

In small, cooperative groups, the class investigated different ways they could get others involved and influence them to support their cause. Faced with analyzing several pages, the students took the assignment seriously, taking turns reading sections and preparing to present their findings to the whole class.

The text was an affirmation of many of their own ideas. This excited them, since they were reading about many practices in the book. One student commented, "We are good 'cause we already doing all these things!" The students celebrated that their actions were purposeful and similar to the methods of organizing outlined by experts.

Responses and Lack Thereof

Other schools and classes began to get involved and participate in parts of our action plan. After learning about the Carr students' work, one school in the northern Chicago suburbs decided to write letters advocating for their

Cabrini Green counterparts. As a result, correspondence between the two classes continued, and the suburban fifth graders decided to make a newspaper featuring the work of my students. A nearby private school in the city also got involved. High school juniors studying school funding issues paid Room 405 a visit and began writing letters, making posters, and collecting signatures as well. Astonished by the poor facilities at Carr, these affluent students had big ideas to help the cause and wanted to expand the initiative.

With suburban and private school students getting involved in the class's efforts, there were intriguing racial and class dynamics at play. The Room 405 students exposed their affluent peers to the reality of school funding issues and the marginalization they faced in their classroom. Alarmed by what they witnessed, the fellow students, attending schools with seemingly unlimited resources, decided to take action on behalf of the Carr students. Through dialogue and firsthand shared experiences, all the students were able to engage in active democratic participation to make change, bridging race and class divisions. Ironically, while many outsiders were getting involved, the Room 405 students were having difficulty in making contact with the school system decision makers.

After no response to their formal paper letters, Chester and Reggie decided to send e-mails. There was no response from these e-mails either, until Chester added to the top of his electronic correspondence, "Our class is disappointed we had not heard from you about our letter. Please respond to the letter we sent to you a very long time ago. We hope to hear from you soon."

Finally, after much persistence, responses arrived from the district's high-ranking officials. An administrative assistant to one executive wrote to say that the central office had received their inquiry in late February and needed time to investigate what current improvements were planned for Carr. In closing, she thanked them for sharing their concerns but asked for patience.

The students were perplexed by the need to wait longer. Excited to have finally received some correspondence, they were also exasperated with the fact that the situation at Carr Academy needed to be investigated. One student called out, "That's not right. There is nothing to investigate— alls they need to do is come here or look at our photos or walk down the halls to see that this place is messed up!" A day later, the class received another e-mail from a different high-ranking Chicago Public Schools decision maker. This note also indicated that the problems identified were being looked into and promised a follow-up response from the official once information had been gathered.

Again, the mood of the classroom was less than receptive to this note. Students wondered out loud, "Why don't they just come out here? They can do all the checking here." The students were right; they had done a lot of checking, researching, and investigating and presented the school's inadequacies quite clearly. Although a response was promised in both e-mails, it would be months before we would hear from the decision makers again.

Even though desired news wasn't coming from the district's top brass, the class was in full gear. Instead of spending our days in periods for each subject, as is typical of most schools, the classroom curriculum clearly had evolved. The school day was now consistently encompassed entirely by this project. Room 405 was certainly no longer a regular classroom; it had taken on the designation of *Project Citizen Headquarters*.

Getting the Video Documentary Started

Tavon was set on putting together a video documentary and had rallied several classmates. As he stated in his journal, "Making a documentary . . . is important because we can show it to somebody and they can tell somebody else and get a whole thing started. People seeing videos of our school can't disagree we need a new one."

As I could not offer Tavon guidance in creating a video, I encouraged him to contact the teacher's aide who worked with the video club. Frustrated by his lack of response, and without my knowledge, Tavon contacted Karen Percak, a familiar resource from the Collaboratory. He poignantly e-mailed her, "We want to make a video documentary. Will you come to our school to help us? We know you are good at them!"

Showing up just days later, Karen began working with a small team of self-selected students during the last days of February. She taught them the entire process from storyboarding and scheduling interviews to editing. The experience was comprehensive. As one team member remarked, "We had to plan it all out. . . . There was a lot of work to do." Tavon reflected, "Today our group had interviewed 9 people. We worked with Ms. Percak for hours. She had her video camera with her. . . . The interview was good and I think it is going to help."

An important part of this experience was that the students realized they had more knowledge and skills than I did with this phase of the project.

The group eagerly demonstrated to the rest of the class, including me, what they had learned, essentially teaching us about making videos. It was exciting and novel for me to watch the student-created and -directed documentary. Perhaps given the chance, we would have the next Steven Spielberg or Spike Lee in the making.

JUST LIKE A RECORD DEAL

The students scoured the Internet to find additional influential people to whom they could send their letter. In classroom conversations, we talked extensively about decision makers in the local government. Each student was on a mission to get the word out to anyone who could help us get a new school. We had brainstormed for politically powerful people. Several of them saw the task as competitive, and their lists began to grow. By the end of the hourlong session, several students were bragging, as some had found as many as 30 names and addresses.

The compiled list included everyone from Vice President Dick Cheney to local legislators and even candidates running for the U.S. Senate from Illinois. Local news organizations and various media contacts were added, as the students believed this would be the best way to inform others about their plight. With a list of almost 200 individuals, Tavon and Dyneisha were eager to stay after school to do the tedious task of transcribing their peers' writing onto envelopes.

The next day there was still more work to do. Some students had only been able to get e-mail addresses. The class decided to use the same letter for the e-mails that they had used for the regular mail. It was also determined that each e-mail letter still needed an appropriate salutation. As one student noted, "Ain't no one want to get no letter that don't have they name on it." The e-mails went out one by one. Questions fluttered around the room about how long it would take before people responded. I was curious, too, and wondered if this letter, written by fifth graders, was going to get responses at all.

It did not take long to have our questions answered. The following Tuesday morning several messages stamped March 1st were waiting in the students' inbox. The first was a form response from a state senator: "Thanks for recent correspondence. . . . Your opinion will receive careful consideration when the issue is presented in the Senate." As Jaris read the response to the quietly awaiting class, another student shouted, "That message bogus! He ain't writin' to us. He says that to everyone." He was exactly right. Unfortunately, their first taste of a response was typical of an elected official: removed and insincere. But the second e-mail was better, promising a visit from State Representative Willie Delgado and stating, "I would be glad to visit your school. The conditions that you described should not exist in America today . . . I will do whatever I can to make sure that the board of education, and the State of Illinois address these concerns."

"Do you really think he's gonna do anything for us?" Terrance skeptically cried out.

Even with the disbelief, there was a sense the class was getting somewhere. They had made a connection. Someone on their list was actually interested in them! Responding to the e-mail, the students made fists, banging them together—a sort of high-five I might have done 20 years earlier when I was their age. Although they had searched for important people they wanted on their side, they were not exactly aware of what a representative did or how he could help them. What they did know was that he was coming to Carr and they had better begin investigating.

Another exciting communication arrived the very next day from *Chicago Tribune* columnist Eric Zorn, who replied to the students' query: "I'm very interested in what you're telling me and would like to arrange to visit you to talk about this situation more."

That evening I spoke with Zorn by phone. We discussed the project and the students' efforts thus far. As I spoke to "the real deal," as students referred to him, Zorn was eager to talk with the kids to, as he said, "See for myself." He assured me he was interested in writing a story; it just had to be postponed until he could clear his desk of current stories he was covering.

My principal needed to be approached about the prospects. Fully aware of the project, the principal had been extremely encouraging, but up to now the hype was mostly contained within the school. This was a sensitive topic, and a newspaper article could stir things up in the city and at the board of education. Although the principal had been fighting this same cause for years, I wanted to prepare him for the potential buzz and backlash. I knew he had supported the project, but how far was he going to allow the students and me to take it? Would he actually let the story get into the mainstream press? What might the repercussions be?

Without hesitation, he approved. He supported the students' efforts because, as he said, "It is appropriate for me to back them since they are doing something to help themselves." With his permission, I was excited to tell the class about my conversation with both Zorn and the principal.

After my announcement, one child shouted out, "That's right, that's right, they all gonna want to talk to us!" Another commented, "That cool . . . we gonna get plastered all over that paper and it's gonna get us a whole new school!" Although there was the expectation of instant gratification, the students were forced to wait several weeks for Zorn to visit the classroom. As we waited, the students looked in other directions to continue their quest.

Days later, a student came in early with an idea. Tyrone told me he had "been watchin' TV news last night with my mama" and had seen "something about the upcoming U.S. Senate race." His idea was that "if these people running wanted to really help out kids in the state, they would come get us a new school." Obviously, it was not that easy, but his naiveté was endearing. After I directed the boy to a few Web pages about the approaching primary, he was able to gather a list of candidates to whom he promptly forwarded the class's letter.

There were responses within hours. One primary candidate, Jeffrey Ruiz, responded to the subject "Our school NEEDS your help" by explaining his past role in trying to secure a new Carr school: "I visited Carr Academy many times and know that you need a new school to learn better. When I was working as [a high-ranking official at] the Chicago School Board, we planned to replace Carr Academy . . . however, I left that position before work began." Intrigued by his knowledge of Carr, the students continued reading:

> I'm sorry to say that I do not know why the new Carr school has not yet been built. I am currently running for the U.S. Senate, where I will fight for the money to build new schools across this country. There are lots of schools like Carr Academy and many students just like you need a better school. I am sorry that I cannot come visit Carr at this time. My election is soon and I am working very hard to win.

By the end of his e-mail, many students argued about whether he might be partially to blame that the school never got built. "Why is he apologizing?" asked one boy.

"If he couldn't get Carr built, how's he think he can get schools all over the country built?" another added.

As I listened to the commentary about Ruiz's letter, I sensed a condescending tone. To me, the candidate's response was problematic: Rather than commending the Carr students for taking action by reaching out to people they thought could help them, he implied that the Carr students were just like other students in need of better schools.

Building on the comments of the students, I also believed the letter showed a level of ignorance on this candidate's part. The students were fully aware of what was occurring around them, especially in terms of gentrification. Ruiz acted uninformed by not attempting to address this issue. Did he think the students were incapable of participating in such a discussion? Was he willing to participate in such a discussion? Frustrated with the lack of resolve, the students, however, did heed his closing advice "to keep working for a new school" with or without his assistance. And, even though their initial response appeared to be negative, the students understood that a quick response from a Senate candidate at least showed respect for them.

Ruiz was a very familiar name in the Chicago school district. He had been a high-ranking official for years. My principal had dealt with him directly on many issues, noting that Ruiz had promised, in writing, that there would be a new Carr school built on an adjacent plot of land six years earlier. Students were also painfully aware that the construction had not begun. They passed daily by the misleading propaganda at the proposed new school site; a sign proclaiming the "New Carr" was continually tagged with graffiti "NOT!!" scribbled across the false promise.

Later that day, as I waited for students to trek across the street, returning from the borrowed gym—one of the central problems with the school, according to the students—the principal called me for an impromptu meeting. He explained he had just spoken to a gentleman describing himself as the campaign manager for Jeffrey Ruiz. The principal's apprehension was obvious as he handed me a pink message slip. Apparently, Ruiz's campaign manager had pitched the idea of a visit to our fifth-grade classroom. My principal questioned Ruiz's motives for the proposed visit and discussed his skepticism.

Although I wanted to respect the principal's wishes, I felt strongly that neither he nor I could make this decision without consulting the students. I was certain he did not want me to bring it up with the class, but I was passionate about letting them solve this problem. If I was presenting the project as theirs, I needed to really live the ideals and could not relent when the going got tough or when a hard "adult decision" needed to be made. Due to my own curiosity, allegiance, and commitment to scaffolding the democratic classroom, I needed to at least return the campaign manager's call to find out more details about his intentions.

That evening I called the campaign manager. Sounding rushed, he explained, "Ruiz wants to show he is involved in the community. He wants to have television cameras come for a photo opportunity. In addition to bringing the publicity to the kids' project," he explained, "Ruiz wants to present the children with a $500 check—a gesture he realizes won't get a new school but would show he wants to give back to the community."

As I listened quietly without comment, I now understood the principal's reservations about the proposition. Intuition told me the motives were self-directed and political, but I was determined not to make the decision for my students. They were the ones who had reached out, and they should be the ones to respond. But at what cost?

During a sleepless night, I tried to weigh the pros and cons of the situation. I certainly did not want the children exploited for Ruiz's political gain. The principal did not want me to tell them about Ruiz's offer. I was in conflict: Should I follow the wishes of my very supportive administrator, or should I follow the progressive curriculum I had created with the students? Even though I was uncomfortable with the offer, the decision had to be left to the kids. I was in the midst of creating a justice-oriented, democratic classroom in which the students' voices and opinions really counted, and I needed to stick with this intention.

The next morning, when the class had settled in, I explained that Principal Miller had received a call from one of the Senate campaign offices to which the class had sent their letter. I explained that I had returned the call the prior evening and learned some valuable information that I knew they would be interested in hearing.

As I presented what I had discovered, I tried to remain neutral and simply present the facts. It was difficult. I had pressure from the administration not to present the offer at all. Likewise, I believed the students' decision making would be worth the gamble and wanted them to have the opportunity to sort it out. What if they were not able to see the offer as the principal and I had? As much as I did not want to give up the authority of my classroom and believed I knew what was best for them, it could not be my decision.

As the classroom teacher, I had the power to make the decision, but now I was yielding that power to the students. This authority was something that I felt I had earned over the past two years, and because of the desire to create a democratic space, I was attempting dangerous teaching by relinquishing it. This was one of the hardest decisions I had to make.

I presented the details of the telephone call. As I outlined the facts, I was quickly interrupted by the students' excitement. "We can buy an X-Box,

PlayStation, or GameCube for the classroom with all that cash!" one exclaimed. Another advocated for "pizza every day." I could understand the excitement; I had felt the same sort of energy when I first heard the news. When I asked for a decision, almost every student voted to accept Ruiz's offer. Each child also had an idea of how to spend the money to improve the school.

Above the din of the deliberations, Crown, a student who rarely participated in class discussions, strained to be heard. Crown stopped the class by raising his voice slightly: "Y'all put down y'all hands 'cause we have to talk 'bout this." Shockingly, he got everyone's attention immediately. I was in awe and envied him. It seemed so easy for him to get control. I really had never seen this side of him and was eagerly waiting to hear his perception.

Crown spoke quietly, almost under his breath, but his voice displayed unbelievable confidence. "You guys really trust this man? How d'ya know he's gonna help us? Instead of thinking it like this dude's comin' in to give us five hundred bucks, let's do some checkin' on him first." The skepticism was not unusual for any of my students. They had often been made empty promises and had often been disappointed. Trust was a big issue for them. But he was not just being reluctant; he had a lot more to say. I took a step back and let Crown have control.

As Crown slumped back into his chair, he directed Tavon over to our working computer. He told Tavon to "Get onto one of them Web sites that has the Senate race stuff on it." Quickly, Crown asked Tavon to find out "who had the most for the race." It was a directive that did not seem to make much sense to many of the students in the room, or me. Was he asking about votes or funding? It did not matter, since Crown had chosen his researcher wisely and they connected. He knew the hand-picked classmate was a math whiz and an expert on the computer and would quickly get the information he was looking for. They traded some comments back and forth, and then Crown said, "He got it" and was ready to continue his sermon, "'Cause that's all I needed to know."

"Listen here," he said. "Let's think about it like a record deal."

I was not sure of his direction, but I was so curious.

"If y'alls wanted a record deal, what label would you want to sign with?" Everyone had given their attention to this boy, and with his ensuing question they all shouted at the tops of their lungs several different popular labels. Through the commotion, I heard Def Jam and Roc-A-Fella. Settling the group down, he continued, "Okay, okay. Me, too, if they came here I would want to be with them, too. But now, what is a record label you would not want anything to do with?" And without hesitation, Darnell blurted out, "Billie Jean." Billie Jean was one of Michael Jackson's record labels. Jackson had recently been on the news due to charges of sexually molesting boys.

It all came quickly together. Crown brought his real-life example of the record label right back to Jeffrey Ruiz's offer. Now sitting up in his chair and using his hands to gesture as he spoke, he eloquently stated, "What Tavon told us about this guy was that he was losing the Senate. There ain't no way this man makin' it to the Senate." He continued his explanation, speaking more emphatically, "He only has 3% of the vote and he can't make it with dat! Listen, it ain't no different than signing with a label. Just like you don't want to be associated with that pervert Michael Jackson, why should we all be associated with this guy who is going to lose?" The faces in front of him had not yet gotten his point, but they remained attentive. "We don't want to go down with his sinkin' ship. If we get seen with him we might never get a new school. Just like you don't want to be hangin' with Michael, we should not want to be with this guy."

It took a few seconds for it to click with his classmates, but then they seemed to understand Crown's explanation and gave some affirming nods. Crown continued:

> And anyway, don't you guys remember that we have that writer from the *Trib* newspaper that wants to do a story on us in a couple weeks? If we take that loser's money it might hurt our chances. I say we hold out for the better deal . . . wouldn't you hold out for the better record deal?

As the class vocally agreed, Crown went on:

> I think this guy is just using us to get in the news heself. He obviously needs something to help and I don't think we should be treated by him. He is just wantin to help out now because it could help him, but lemme tell—ain't nothing gonna help him win his race!

Crown called for a recount. "Who wants this guy to come and mess us up?" Two hands rose against what Crown presented, as one of the students softly voiced that the class could use Ruiz for the cash just as he was using them for his political gain. The rest of the class realized they did not want to be associated with Ruiz based on Crown's creative analogy of the predicament they were in.

It *was* just like a record deal, but I could never have done that. I was in awe.

Just like that, Crown swayed the class's decision on Ruiz. Crown used his charisma and persuasiveness to convince the class based on how he saw the situation. Now the class actually needed to give a response to the offer. We talked about what they would say and even scripted the conversation. Standing at the front of the classroom, Crown used my cell phone to call Ruiz's office. He explained that he was in my class and began to give an explanation that we had rehearsed, but he did not stop there.

The class and I listened as he explained:

> We are very happy that Mr. Ruiz wants to come out and see us at our school, but we think and we voted that he should not come out right now. Since the primary is just a couple of days away we think he may be too busy and it might be too crazy for him to come for a visit right now.

He paused for a response on the other end and then continued:

> We think that it was very nice of him to want to see us and the hard work we are doin' but we don't think it is a good time. We would like to invite Mr. Ruiz to come for a visit after the primary, and if he comes, he doesn't even need to bring us the money.

Crown closed the phone and handed it back to me. He did not say a word, but his smile was so big and so confident it remains vividly etched in my memory.

We never heard from Ruiz or his staff again.

4

Seeking a Perfect Solution

Students interview Illinois Representative Willie Delgado

THE *CHICAGO TRIBUNE*

As promised, about a week after the Senate primary, I received a call from
Eric Zorn of the *Chicago Tribune* to arrange a meeting for a newspaper story.
Although the students' letter and e-mail campaigns were proving successful, there was no mainstream media support yet. Even though Room 405
had anticipated the visit for several weeks, I was extremely nervous about
an article about the project being published.

Exploitation by the media was my ultimate concern. Meeting with
Zorn would be a great opportunity to step up the level of their fight, but
my role was to protect them from the various unknowns of that exposure.
My commitment to the pedagogical ideals of allowing the students to co-
create their learning did not make me sleep any easier. Could letting outsiders into the classroom ultimately hurt their efforts? What were this
reporter's intentions? Despite this uncertainty, I still felt comfortable with
Zorn. He seemed to have integrity, and although I was unsure about the
process, I felt that I could trust him.

The students began to prepare for Zorn when they arrived at Carr early Monday morning. They swept the floor, cleaned the boards, and straightened the desks. They wanted to make a good impression. Others organized their information folders so they could "show off what we've done and get him to sign the petition," as Malik said.

Zorn arrived right on time. He described his role at the *Tribune*, and the students listened attentively. Watching them sit so quietly, I wondered if they were skeptical, like me, about the manner in which he was going to tell their story. Their concern would be no surprise. Cabrini Green was negatively portrayed by the Chicago newspapers weekly, and as Crown told me prior to Zorn's visit, "Us folk always be in the news for bad things."

Following his introduction, Zorn met with a small group of the students in the hallway. It was important to keep the group small and manageable, but who should have the opportunity? This dilemma would continue to confront me throughout the following months as the children continued getting more exposure. I felt that each student should have the chance to tell their story, as everyone was working hard in its pursuit, but some students were better able to talk to adults than others, and I did not want to leave it to chance.

All of the students had shown different strengths along the Project Citizen journey. Some students who struggled with tests and typical indications of learning became the best advocates for their cause, connecting the work to real life. The project was a true testament to multiple intelligences and different ways of learning. Though each student had something to offer, I could only delegate a few students and was concerned with the message my selection would send to those not chosen. Since the discussion was not a traditional assessment, it was an opportunity to go beyond merely choosing the classroom's highest achievers. I chose strong communicators combined with those I felt would benefit from the experience.

Once selected, the group quickly arranged the chairs in a circle. As Zorn asked each of them their names, the students appeared almost embarrassed. They mumbled and in several instances could not be heard. Zorn was unaffected and just continued to scribble his notes. Observing from behind the circle, I watched him vigorously write as each student responded to his queries. He often asked the students for clarification and would then turn to me for further insight. At one point, he asked me to clarify an answer, but before I could respond, Dyneisha interrupted stating, "It's our interview, and you should be quiet!" I was glad they were taking control even though they lost track of chronology and had difficulty staying focused.

They were more interested in showing the school's deficiencies than in retelling their attempts to solve the problem. They all talked at once. I struggled with trying to get some control and even caught myself giving students the "teacher eye." Zorn saw my intervention and encouraged their energy, remarking that he "liked the idea of debate and discourse, as it helps flesh out the issues and bring the most important and passionate things forward."

After he had finished with the students, he asked me very pointed questions. Zorn focused on me more than I would have liked. Heeding Dyneisha's advice, I tried to redirect him toward the students, since I wanted him to know that the whole effort was coming from them. Even though I felt that I had no choice but to respond when he asked me anything directly, I wanted the kids to tell the story in their own words.

Malik offered Zorn his information packet: "You could look at all the surveys, writings, and pictures once you get back to your office to write since . . . this might help you if you forget anything." Zorn willingly accepted the student-created booklet containing everything from temperature charts and petitions to survey results and interview forms.

After the interview, Zorn toured the school for almost an hour, examining all of the students' complaints. Next, he spoke with the school administrators and the engineer and requested the contact information for the Local School Council president. He informed me of his plans to visit both nearby Cresswell Elementary and the empty lot to view the sign proclaiming the planned new Carr.

I was impressed by his diligence. As he was leaving, he told me how impressed he was with the students' efforts to identify the problem and systematically solve it and how he looked forward to putting all the pieces together. "Hopefully," he commented, "I will have the article in tomorrow's paper."

That evening Zorn called to tell me there was both good and bad news. The good news was that the article was going to be in the paper the next day, but the bad news was his discovery: "There is a no-go on the new school. From my conversations with the chief operations officer at the school board," Zorn said, "I learned the Carr operation will be moved over to Cresswell."

My initial frustration turned to anger. How had he gotten in touch with the officer so effortlessly? The students had been unsuccessful in their attempt to reach him for weeks via telephone calls, letters, and e-mails.

Perhaps this was perfect timing. If the students were agitated by Zorn's grim news, their scheduled interview for the next day with the self-proclaimed radical teacher Therese Quinn might have been just what was necessary to transform their fight into public action. Quinn, a community activist and university professor at Chicago's School of the Art Institute, was a promising resource for the students to engage with since part of her work focuses on how young people can gain access to resources so they can fully participate in aspects of our democracy. Wasn't it fitting that they would learn how to become activists themselves? Little did I realize the way the students would respond to the article when it appeared in print.

Taking public transportation to the school, I stopped at newsstands along the way to get enough copies of the *Tribune* for each student. When the first student found the article on the front page of the second section, he shouted, "Found it! March 23, 2004, 'Pupils Welcome All to See Their Dreary Reality.' Go to section B at the top to read 'bout us!" I watched each child find the article and begin reading. Some read silently, while others stumbled over some words as they read aloud line by line. There was definite excitement as they went through the sentences looking to get the meaning of the article as they searched for their own quotes.

I remember enthusiastically watching these fifth graders enjoying reading. Individually, each student took the initiative to get through the entire article; each had a stake in what it said. They all wanted to read what that guy wrote about them and see their efforts headlined in the newspaper.

Tavon and his video documentary team had arranged for Karen Percak from the Collaboratory, along with a videographer, to be present for the interview of activist Therese Quinn later in the morning. It was a bonus to get footage of the first deconstruction of an article about them in a newspaper.

As we went through the text, we were able to talk about personification, albeit in a manner unconventional when compared to a traditional language arts curriculum. The article contained a real-life example of the literary device: "Cresswell Academy of the Arts, a recently built $15 million facility that sits in mocking splendor just across a ball field from Carr" (Zorn, 2004a, p. B1). Definitions had to be found for the great new vocabulary found in the article. The key to reading and making sense of the article was that these students—students who were labeled as incapable, not meeting standards, at risk, and struggling—were readily able to make sense of what they read. They were able to decipher the meanings from context, just by looking around the room as Zorn did the previous day. They may have stumbled over some words, but they understood, made sense of, and connected with the text! They consulted the dictionary when a word surpassed their vocabularies because they truly wanted to know the meaning. The text was alive; it was about them.

Most of the students were engaged in the reading lesson, and my initial reservations about having the videographer present and not wanting to be caught on tape being a bad teacher subsided. Classroom management, luckily, was not difficult because the students were genuinely interested in the material and remained focused.

Although the reading went well, I was concerned during the activity. In my journal I wrote,

> I was originally frustrated because I thought that Demetrius was joking around during the article discussion. What I had failed to realize was that while we were analyzing the text, Demetrius had found another article that was totally relevant to us.

While the class was working on the Zorn article, he had read about the governor's proposed dismantling of the Illinois State Board of Education and dedicating the funds—$2.2 billion—to individual districts for school construction. As he pointed and made noises to get others' attention about the adjacent article, he was raising the issue of whether this money could help get a new school built for Carr. Like many teachers, I simply ignored what seemed like an interruption.

Reflecting on this now, it is very telling about what I thought my role was in the classroom. As the teacher, I needed to maintain some sense of the control. Apparently, I was not willing to allow Demetrius to fully embody the democratic principles I strived for. What I initially failed to see would actually have added significant value to the discussion.

When I realized my mistake, I backed off, allowing Demetrius to take the curriculum into his own hands. His discovery allowed us to expand the conversation to issues of power, race, and school funding. He wanted to know why, if the government had so much money to spend, it was not fixing up Carr. He raised the issue—loud and clear—to his classmates, wondering why their needs were being ignored. He asked, "Is it 'cause we Black and poor that nobody wants to help us?" As the students left the text of the Zorn article and tackled the highly political topic, I was intrigued by their ability to connect current events to the context of their learning.

After this intense discussion, we returned to the Zorn article: "The bad news for the pupils is that, this year, money is finally on the way to fix some of the cosmetic issues—the perpetually foggy windows, for instance—that give their plight such poignancy" (Zorn, 2004a, p. B1).

I can still hear Dyneisha shouting, "Mr. Schultz, you just makin' us waste our breath!" She was totally exasperated, as were her classmates when they read the lines. Dyneisha's frustration couldn't have been articulated more clearly. She did not want just some things to get fixed because then some of the school's biggest shortcomings—like the lack of a lunchroom, gym, or auditorium—could never be remedied. For some, this assessment was a good thing, but any sense of goodness was squelched as they read on:

> This is bad news because it signals . . . the school system is no longer in a position to spend another $15 million. . . . Given the declining enrollment trends due to gentrification, Cresswell school will ultimately absorb Carr's population. (Zorn, 2004a, p. B1)

There was a new intensity in the room. It was a combination of frustration and disappointment. Malik said pointedly, "We done with this Project Citizen. It's over; we ain't getting no school! I am retiring from Project Citizen." With that, he threw down his red project folder. The energy and mood in the room had quickly changed.

I shared my point of view and tried to explain to the students how I interpreted the article. I was able to connect with some, showing that there weren't any new developments in the article. Their retorts showed annoyance, since they had not heard from an operations officer, and, as one said, "This guy got him to talk right away." There was discussion that nobody was listening to children and that this whole thing was a big waste of time. I understood their irritation, but the biggest disappointment was that the article told them they were going to end up at Cresswell. All the choices previously afforded them were quickly stripped away when they read these words in print. Even though there was a lot of anger in the room, it was an opportunity to revisit how and why things are written.

Whereas attending Cresswell—a shiny, expensive new school—would appear to have been excellent news, a transfer to this nearby school was much more complicated. Carr families had cultivated a school community over the decades in which they had tremendous pride. Parents (and grand-parents) did whatever it took to ensure their children's attendance at Carr, even amid displacement out of the school's neighborhood boundaries. Although just across a ball field from each other, historically Cresswell and Carr had been adversaries. Although the rivalry had not been as pronounced in recent years, the family loyalty to the schools was still intense; thus, the article's findings were not welcome news.

YOUNG WARRIORS

This project had already exceeded my wildest expectations, and it was successful even if the students did not proceed any further. The students, however, still had important tasks previously arranged for the day and, surprisingly, wanted to carry them out. What had appeared to be a consensus to throw in the towel dissipated, and the group that had arranged for the video team and for an interview continued in their roles. Even though several members of the video team had voiced their outrage, they forged ahead and completed a two-hour tour of the building with their guests. Every nook and cranny in the building was taped, and several interviews were conducted. The professional videographer allowed the students to "use his real-deal equipment and trusted all of us with it," Reggie announced proudly.

This idea of trust was something that I had been trying to develop with my students throughout my teaching. I was impressed with their sophisticated conversations about trust. They were pleased to get it, wanted to share it, and used it to get what they wanted. Room 405 students felt their efforts were allowing them to trust more as they spoke to more people and got others involved.

Weeks of planning culminated in another trust-related situation when Therese Quinn visited. The kids had been extremely excited to talk with her about the different ways she had taken action and were wondering if they could adopt her tactics to help them get a new school.

While Therese told them stories, they became quite noisy. The students eagerly called out, asking probing questions about her organizing experiences. I was noticeably frustrated and wanted the students to calm down, but Therese assured me that she was comfortable with and welcomed what she called enthusiasm.

Students discuss strategies with Therese Quinn in Room 405.

As she proceeded through her stories, she presented different means of getting the word out to make a statement. Instead of a classroom interview, the students and Therese had a group discussion. When she mentioned her ideas, the students added their own. She suggested they "go to a school nicer than Carr and demand you attend." As the ideas floated about, one student called out that "it would be cool to block the elevators at the BOE [Board of Education]," while another shouted, "Let's take it to the street . . . we should go on strike and demonstrate. Forget this school!"

"There ain't no way that I'm demonstratin'; the cops will hurt us," Tyrone responded to the suggestion. It was a perfect opportunity for a talk about how they could organize and march. Therese was able to speak of demonstrating and notifying the media about what they had planned. She addressed head-on their concerns about police brutality, an area in which I had little experience. My students had legitimate concerns as they detailed how some police officers treated people in the community.

The racial undertone of how urban African Americans are treated was an important phenomenon for the students. It was also something that I could understand only in a secondhand way. Although I could listen to what the students said, I was never going to face what they described. How could I encourage my students to do something that I knew nothing about?

The students laid out their concerns about protesting and demonstrating in light of their own experiences. Therese was able to explain that if they organized their demonstration in a peaceful way, "You should not be afraid that the police would beat you up," because, as she said, "They would not want to be caught on tape doing harm to innocent, nonviolent protestors." She went on to suggest that "the more people you kids get to come out to support you, the police will not harass or threaten you."

Therese encouraged the students to look up some stories about a hunger strike that had occurred in the Chicago's Little Village neighborhood. She began detailing how community members took action by sleeping outside on a proposed school site. Before she could even get the entire story out, Dyneisha interrupted, "Lady, you crazy, there ain't no chance you getting me to sleep outside 'round here. This is Cabrini Green! You can't do that here!" Although there were doubters, others later looked up the stories and learned about how others had been successful in fighting the Chicago school board.

Challenged by some naysayers, Therese offered some sage advice: "The mayor and others would listen to you fifth graders because you have already been so successful. You have gotten so many people to listen to you, and for that you should be proud." With their attention, she continued, "The mayor would not risk looking like a fool in front of all the people and cameras if you decided to do something public." The students understood the importance in her advice.

This visit was different from the others. Instead of talking to the students like an administrative authority, she was able to connect with students from her real-life activist endeavors. She was extremely candid, giving them realistic things to think about. Even though I was able to see this interview as different, I feared that once she left the students would refocus on the "bad news" and that their insatiable desire to challenge the system would be gone.

As I suspected, with Therese no longer fueling their fire, Room 405 lost its energy. The day of several big events and opportunities had ended. Most students left the school in rotten spirits. Was this project of a lifetime finished for all of us? Was it time to try something different?

Little did the students know that after they went home e-mails flooded their inbox. Even though it seemed that they had heard the news so long ago, the public was reacting to the *Tribune* column. The responses would reignite their passions. The correspondence pushed Room 405 to keep up the momentum and continue their fight. One particular letter stood out.

Courage is a Decision
To the students of room 405,

    Do you realize how brave you are in fighting for what is right? Many adults do not dare voice their opinion, but you all took a stand. Please do not give up the fight. Did you know that the civil rights movement in the 1960's was not just led by the adults but by the young people? One group called SNCC—Student Non-violent Coordinating Committee—actually helped black people in Mississippi to win the right to vote in their state. . . . The members of SNCC taught in a "freedom school" and helped youth and adults learn about their rights as citizens. These young people worked hard and sometimes felt like giving up but they were determined to make a difference and stand up for what was right. So stay strong, young warriors your ancestors would be very proud of you!!

                                      Cassandra McKay

As the students entered the classroom the next day, their confidence seemed gone until we read the McKay e-mail aloud. Their demeanors instantly changed. I hurried the students to the computer lab so they could capture the ideas fresh in their minds, as there was an obvious renewal to their vigor.

Their journal entries reflected the power of this short note. The students latched onto each word and allowed the message to resonate. Tavon wrote, "We can make a difference in our community by working hard. We are never going to give up. . . . Thank you for comparing us to freedom fighters . . . like King and student[s] of SNCC."

Having learned about African American history year after year, they relished the thought of being compared to their heroes. It was extremely powerful for all of us. The call to fight was heard loud and clear, as was apparent in Dyneisha's writing:

This mean a lot to me noing that you care. . . . I am proud of my self and my mother and father is to . . . because this is 11-year-olds trying to make it write in there community. . . . Please keep in couraging us.

Shaniqua also brought up issues relating to her family supporting her:

We probably won't give up. we are going to keep our heads up. My family is so happy that I been keeping up the good working and they told me the same thing you told me to be brave and to stand up for what you work for and be strong.

This short letter raised the issue of pride, self-worth, and respect. It made the students realize they were making a difference. Dyneisha was concerned about what she could do for the greater good of her community, while Shaniqua recognized that the work she was doing was exceeding all sorts of expectations. I was struck by the way both girls felt that it was important to bring issues of family values and doing good work into the classroom. McKay's letter made all the students examine where they stood in regard to what they wanted from the project. Whereas the girls showed a sense of strength in moving forward, Reggie was particularly affected by the connection to the civil rights movement:

> Now I am going to fight for what is right to get a new school. We are not going to give up the fight for nothing. We can be brave for a new school like the SNCC. . . . We were like young warriors and our ancestors would be very proud. This makes me feel much better because I want to keep fighting. I was upset and mad yesterday because of what was written in the newspaper . . . your letter makes me want to go on.

Jaris read further into the correspondence, delving into the broader meaning behind the letter, asking: "When you said our ancestors will be proud if we keep figthing but if we stop figthing do you think our ancestors will be mad?"

Each student connected with the McKay note in remarkable ways. They took it seriously because they were being taken seriously. This simple letter gave more encouragement than any motivational speech I could have made.

CARR'S "SAVAGE INEQUALITIES"

As Demetrius continued reading, "Soap, paper towels and toilet paper are in short supply. There are two working bathrooms for some 700 children" (Kozol, 1992, p. 63). Terrance called out, "This guy must've seen Carr!" As a class, we were reading a chapter in Jonathan Kozol's *Savage Inequalities*. The students were working hard to deconstruct Kozol's text, which was now over a decade old. Even though it may have been dated, the students sitting in Room 405 thought it was a precise portrayal of their school. Kozol had spent two years visiting schools around the country in the late 1980s. Although it was a chore to work through a text written for adults, the class persevered. As the students struggled through the chapter together, they found it unbelievably detailed and specific to their cause. They connected many of the descriptions to their own work and to their school; they became increasingly infuriated by their situation.

In a section of the chapter entitled "Other People's Children," the students learned why schools in the suburbs were getting better resources. The students were interested in this topic after comparing resources between schools in different areas of Chicago and across the country. They were frustrated that some schools were nice and neat, while others were all messed up.

Chester read aloud from Kozol: "The answer is found, at least in part, in the arcane machinery by which we finance public education. Most public schools in the United States depend for their initial funding on a tax on local property" (p. 54). Chester continued, "[city schools] are likely to end up with far less money for each child in their schools. . . . 30 percent or more of the potential tax base (in larger cities like Chicago) is exempt from taxes" (p. 55). At this point, several students looked up, frustrated by what they heard. Before Chester could even finish the page, a full-fledged class discussion began that connected back to what Demetrius had discovered weeks earlier when the class read Zorn's article. Although many words were unknown, the students got the essence. Kozol, indeed, was describing Carr.

When reading Kozol's words, "Equity, after all, does not mean simply equal funding" (p. 54), the students began discussing ways they could advocate to change this situation. The students used the Socratic method, a pedagogical approach that gives students questions to ponder rather than providing answers in a lecture-style format. This teaching style promotes critical thinking, inquiry, and reasoning among students. As subject matter or texts are probed for meaning, a discussion among the participants can be achieved. These skills allowed the students to glean the meaning out of text at multiple levels. My training with the Great Books Foundation on how to conduct this type of shared inquiry proved to be very beneficial (http://www.greatbooks.org). Rather than having one right answer, shared inquiry allowed students to rely directly on the text to interpret meaning for themselves, essentially inviting them to discuss their findings, and disagreements, with each other.

Throughout the year, the students had become comfortable with this approach, and now that it was near the end of March, I was always amazed to hear fifth graders utilizing these strategies to get their points heard. Prior to learning this technique, Dyneisha, for instance, would dominate class discussions. Now, without interrupting her peers, she said with a deep breath, "I agree with Tavon, but everyone needs to turns back to page 54 'cause you will see that there is more to it." As the others in the class followed her cue, she repeated what had been read by another classmate several minutes earlier, "How can it be that inequities as great as these exist in neighboring school districts?" (p. 54). As she recited these lines aloud, she explained her idea.

I was certainly willing to allow her to proceed on her tangent after what I learned from Crown and his record-deal analogy. Dyneisha explained that when Willie Delgado, representative to the Illinois House, came tomorrow we should ask him about these funding questions. She continued, saying that he should provide them with answers about these issues and maybe help us get our new school. She said, "We should give that Willie Delgado guy all of the letters we be getting and then ask him about the money!"

I had allowed the students to drive the discussion, and I was happy that she and others were connecting the various project entities together. With all the positive letters telling them how smart, creative, and talented they were, it was no surprise that Kamala remarked, "I never cared about the mail at my house before, and now I cannot wait to get stuff here at school every day!"

From an educational standpoint, this correspondence provided a never-ending source of authentic reading and writing, as well as great compliments. There was no need to force the work on the students; the students were taking control of their own learning because it all had a central theme and was all geared toward their ultimate shared goal.

When the first elected official, State Representative Willie Delgado, came to visit the school, the class was interested in what he had to offer, especially in light of the issues Dyneisha had raised. Dyneisha designated herself the lead interviewer. She used her interview guide and developed additional questions to address the inequities the students had uncovered.

"We are studying the problem about our community, about our school being messed up and stuff. What can be done?" Dyneisha asked Representative Delgado.

After attentively listening, Delgado responded, "I am not surprised . . . because I was a student . . . from a real poor community. I went to a school just like yours. That does not mean we are idiots or we should be treated less than anyone else. We are all still human beings."

Immediately connecting with the students by sharing the pain of growing up in a poor community, he portrayed his own childhood in a similar
light to what many in the class had experienced. He won them over instantly, and they willingly remained involved in the interview, probing
with follow-up questions about inequity in schools and wondering how
they could take action.

In response, Delgado commented, "The action that you have taken,
even though you cannot touch and cannot hug it yet, to get our attention,
you have done more than most people do in their entire life!" He continued praising and congratulating them on their hard work and, most important, treating them with genuine respect as if they were adults.

As I looked around the room, each student was holding his or her head
up high in response to Delgado. As Dyneisha continued her questioning,
Delgado was able to step up his rhetoric to deal with some of the race and
class issues she was raising. "It should not be this way . . . the public schools
for our kids, kids of color should not be this way!" exclaimed Delgado,
making sure to stress, "The content of your character is the most important thing."

As he passionately expressed his disdain and "shame on the grownups for building million-dollar homes and not taking care of a school," the
students were able to hear a legislator's perspective on the gentrification
and urban renewal they were witnessing. During his time in Room 405, he
pushed the students to examine the issues surrounding change in the neighborhood, ultimately ending his comments with, "What about you?" His
call for action showed his support for their cause. He told them how he
was going to raise the issue with the school board and question them as to
why they were not responding to the students. Before going on a building
tour, Delgado praised the students "on their bang-up job" and encouraged
them to "keep fighting because you are right." Perhaps his most powerful
statement on the tour came as he walked into the girls' bathroom: "There
are not doors on the stalls and nothing to keep you sanitary? How can we
expect young ladies to become women if this is what we give them? This
makes me sick!"

The visit of Delgado made the students eager to bring other legislators into the classroom, including the chairperson of the education committee for the Illinois State Senate, who was scheduled to visit the following
week.

That the children connected with Delgado was evident in their journals because he told them to "never give up," that he "was very impressed

Students discuss budget plans with Illinois State Senator and
Chairperson of the Education Committee Miguel del Valle.

with us," and because he "knew about and has come to the Greens [Cabrini
Green]." Delgado had also made an impression on me. In my journal I wrote
that it was so neat to see him so passionate with the kids; he had lived their
life and was able to relate.

While the students invited legislators in, I was invited to present the
class's work to the board of directors at the Constitutional Rights Foundation Chicago, the local organization sponsoring Project Citizen. Following
my visit, several board members began corresponding with the students.
This excerpt from a particular e-mail provided the opportunity to discuss
what might happen if we did not get the new school:

> Your commitment to this project is outstanding. You are right to want to
> be in an environment that is more effective for your learning needs. . . .
> The most important thing I have learned is to keep working towards what
> you think is the right solution. If you don't reach the "perfect" solution
> you had originally intended, I have learned that spectacular things
> happen along the way and superb alternatives also appear. . . . While you
> seek a better environment for your education, it seems as though you
> have already, through your own efforts, elevated your education.

The students loved the letter and felt it brought up great topics to discuss. It was perfect timing to have somebody raise the idea of not reaching
our "perfect solution." How would I deal with the consequences associated
with their authentic problem solving if they did not attain their goal? This

was not the safe, fixed consequences found in textbooks. Although there could certainly be disappointment at a less than desired outcome, the students were able to acknowledge the many achievements they had already accumulated. Many were able to recognize these "superb alternatives" that had already appeared, As Reggie wrote, "If we do not get a new school we still learn something about how to have a pitition and do a survey."

Likewise, Dyneisha reflected,"We have learned great things and things are starting to happen even if it aint no new school."

Diminor commented about the publicity associated with their efforts: "We was on the news and in the papers showing what was wrong with the building and we be spectacular."

Artell agreed, "I get to do things that I didnt do be for."

In addition, Jaris recognized that, "If we do not reach the perfect solution I think we can still learn alot."

The students collectively communicated that they knew great things were happening regardless of the end result. They were in touch with their learning and understood that they were experiencing new and different things even if they had not achieved their original goal.

An example of one great alternative outcome was when the class received a letter from the Office of Vice President Cheney. The letter, stamped with an official seal, was specific to the students' request. The letter, dated March 30, 2004, detailed that the vice president's office was forwarding the matter on to the U.S. Department of Education (DOE). The correspondence explained the DOE would immediately review the facts, begin a case, and respond directly to the students.

The kids were elated that the "VP had actually cared 'bout us at Carr!"

But I was skeptical. It seemed like a public relations reply. I kept my private thoughts to myself rather than sharing my doubt with students. About two weeks later, however, to my surprise the students received correspondence directly from the U.S. Department of Education as promised. The DOE had indeed started a case, W.H. ID-WH144524, addressing the specifics of the initial inquiry.

Although much of the content of the letter presented very little new information to them, they were excited that the Department of Education knew about the problems at Carr. Attention from the federal level was a real victory, and I was sincerely impressed by the high-level government accountability in responding to the fifth graders' letter.

With such important documents, the students realized that they needed to gather all the collected information in one location. This need for organization led to another "superb alternative," the Room 405 Web site. Important

UNITED STATES DEPARTMENT OF EDUCATION

OFFICE OF THE DEPUTY SECRETARY

APR 1 5 2004
W.H. ID - WH144524

The Fifth Graders in Room 405

████████████████████████

Chicago, IL 60610

Dear Fifth Graders:

Thank you for your letter to Vice President Richard B. Cheney regarding the need for a new school facility to house the █████████████████████████. We appreciate hearing your concerns. The White House has referred your letter to the Department of Education for review, and I am pleased to respond.

I read your very detailed description of the many problems and limitations of your existing school building, and I certainly understand your desire for a new school. I also appreciate the efforts of your class to learn about our government and help bring about change through Project Citizen.

One fact you may have learned about our system is that the three major levels of government traditionally have had different areas of responsibility. For example, the federal government is largely responsible for national defense, while local governments generally maintain police forces to help ensure safety and order in our local communities.

Under our system of education, state and local governments have primary responsibility for financing and administering elementary and secondary education. The limited role of the federal government has been targeted to helping States and school districts meet the instructional needs of special populations, such as economically disadvantaged students and students with disabilities, and not on basic functions such as maintaining, renovating, or building schools.

You already may have learned that the Chicago Public Schools began an extensive capital improvement program several years ago that aims to renovate or replace decaying school facilities. Under this program, almost $700 million is budgeted during the current year to reduce overcrowding, improve the physical condition of existing schools, and help bring technology into the classroom. Based on your description of the conditions at the ████████, I would hope and expect that your school is scheduled for renovation or replacement in the very near future.

Thank you again for your letter, and I hope each of you continues to take an active role as citizens and future voters in our democratic government.

Sincerely,

Thomas P. Skelly
Director, Budget Service

400 MARYLAND AVE., S.W. WASHINGTON, D.C. 20202-0500
www.ed.gov

Our mission is to ensure equal access to education and to promote educational excellence throughout the Nation.

information and documentation could be easily found and shared with visiting guests, various correspondents, and other interested parties.

After selecting a design for their Web site that everybody agreed on, including using graffiti-style letters for the name of the Web site, the students applied the Project Citizen framework as a way to categorize the entire Web site project: The Problem, The Alternative Solutions, The Class Policy, and The Action Plan.

With help from a fellow doctoral student, and with direction from the kids, we built a comprehensive Web site. Several students worked with me to make sure I was "getting everything in there and doin' it right."

Before the Web site went live, the class debated what to call it. Something related to Project Citizen and Room 405 would yield a unique and original name. In class we went through the Web hosting process and applied for a domain name. Eventually, http://www.projectcitizen405 .com was agreed on.

Once the Web site was launched, the students performed error-testing on all of the pages and created hyperlinks within the site and to other Web sites. The students were reading content all about themselves and enjoying it. Each day, they would compile their recommendations for changes, additions, and corrections, and each evening I would repost their edited documentation.

One of the most memorable additions came from Demetrius. He wanted a better description of the students. On his Addition-Correction Form he wrote, "We need to represent better. We need to be like a family. Add, 'The students all get along. We like each other like brothers and sisters.'" Like a family, they genuinely cared about one another, celebrating successes as they worked together, allowing every member to expand individual horizons to whatever level they were capable. His proposed addition was totally on target.

The students had another reason for celebration: projectcitizen405.com proved to be very successful. It received over 20,000 hits in its first active month. Superb alternatives were occurring daily!

TELEVISION, RADIO, AND PROTECTING THE KIDS

Following the publication of Zorn's article in the *Chicago Tribune*, letters, e-mails, and suggestions started pouring into Headquarters 405. The classroom became a Project Citizen campaign office. Students responded to letters of inquiry, wrote thank-you notes to their supporters, and, of course, continued their research and investigation. The atmosphere in the classroom was intense.

At this point, the students decided to resend their original letter along with the *Chicago Tribune* column to the nonresponding recipients. The students also attempted to indirectly put pressure on the decision makers by contacting the local television stations.

Harry Porterfield of Chicago's ABC affiliate Channel 7 News called within a day of this second mailing. Eager to report the story, Porterfield asked to meet with the students the next day. This posed a problem, as the next day was a teacher professional workshop and students had the day off. How could I guarantee that half a dozen students would show up when they didn't have school? Before I could even think through the logistics, Malik was rallying the troops. He quickly solidified classmates' commitments to join him for the TV cameras.

That evening I spoke to the parents. They were extremely supportive, and some were even a bit starstruck. Hardly able to contain herself,

Dyneisha's mother shouted, "Of course she can come, you makin' my daughter a movie star!" Parents recognized the hard work their children were putting into the project, and they enthusiastically encouraged the work. This attitude was a welcome relief, as the previous year I was constantly being scutinized, even distrusted, as "that new White teacher." With parents involved in the campaign and engaged in their children's schooling, the outside acknowledgment of our efforts increased.

The next day, the students arrived as promised (early in fact), eagerly awaiting the ABC news crew. They were all dressed nicely, especially Dyneisha, with hair freshly braided and wearing a dress—I had never seen her so done-up. Their presentation was certainly reflective of their ambition.

After the television crew arrived, the students led them on a tour of the building, demonstrating the problems of our bedraggled school. As the cameraman filmed, he built a rapport with them, sharing his techniques and answering their questions. Following the tour, Kamala suggested they head over to "where the sign for the new Carr be, 'cause that would be real cool to get on the TV." Heeding Kamala's advice, the television crew visited the adjacent lot. Porterfield ended up introducing the segment for that night's broadcast from the spot.

The television news segment depicted the students' efforts in a historical context. First, the neighborhood was described, and then the long history of gang activity. This background led into details of "the kids on a mission," as the newscaster called them (Shute, 2004).

"There was a time when a brand-new Carr Elementary school was envisioned for this piece of real estate. . . . And that sign marks the spot. The only problem is, the sign is six years old," Porterfield reported.

I was pleased the students were featured on television, since it was a goal of theirs, but was concerned that the historical references might have overshadowed the current efforts. There was so much they were working on, and I wanted to be sure the audience was aware of the students' fight and their struggle. The students, however, loved the news segment. Tyrone commented, "Finally we are getting on the news for something good."

Just days after the class's first television appearance, I received a call from the local NBC affiliate wanting to feature the project. Remembering the excitement from the prior week, coupled with their willingness to come in on a day off, I anticipated the students' fervor and accepted the invitation without reservation. When I broke the news that more TV people would be coming in the next half-hour, the students were completely despondent. Instead of the zealous responses I'd seen before, I was met with frustration and annoyance.

"Why didn't you ask us first?"

"I don't want to be on no more TV!" exclaimed another. The reaction was a complete shock. Now I faced serious resistance that I could not understand.

Shaniqua pulled me aside from the rest of the group and quietly said, "It wasn't cool to not check before you scheduled us up."

She continued as I graciously listened to her mature explanation: "I don't think they don't want to have 'em come but y'know we all needs to be prepared for these things. We gots to look good! You ain't letting us prepare!"

Prepare, huh? I was the one totally unprepared for this! But, hearing Shaniqua's thoughtful insight, I understood the importance of what I had neglected earlier.

Trying to quickly fix the situation, I gathered the group around me in the hallway. I wanted them to know it was okay if we canceled the impending NBC visit. Candidly, I admitted to them, "I made a mistake by not including you in this decision making" and informed them that I would immediately call to change the plans. Despite a few snide comments, many shared Shaniqua's sentiments. They did want this opportunity, but, more important, they wanted to be in control, and they felt betrayed. Once this was out in the open, the students decided to go with my original, but not democratically created, arrangements.

In the 20 minutes they had before the crew's arrival, the students strategized different ways to deal with the TV station. They talked about avoiding the historical overview of the neighborhood. Kamala suggested bringing the architectural plans from the office up to Room 405. Tyrone wanted to show all the letters of support the students had already received. Darnell, Malik, and Dyneisha rehearsed what they might say if they had the chance to be interviewed by the reporter. It was obvious they wanted the perspective to be all about them, and they had ideas of how to achieve this.

Soon, NBC news anchor Anna Davlantes arrived with her crew. She was eager to meet the students and learn about the work that they were doing. I heard one of the students remark, "She really wants to know what we been doin'." Another commented, "She actually listens to what we sayin'." Davlantes spent time with each student: She got a sense of what the students thought about the project, and she allowed them to practice before the camera rolled. She gravitated to two quieter students in particular so she could feature them.

The news feature appearing that evening exemplified a committed journalist who demonstrated her interest in having students heard through the media. Davlantes focused on the problem's severity, how the students were working to solve it, and ways the students were influencing a change for the better. The students' hard work was featured from different angles by the reporters, and they were getting representation from advocating journalists interested in their success. Davlantes articulated this idea that evening: "And, against the backdrop of this dilapidated school, a bright lesson in problem solving these students are not likely to forget" (Piacente, 2004). Viewed as problem solvers interested in bettering their situation, the students were shown as able achievers, learning despite the problems they faced daily.

The publicity regarding the students' work was gaining traction. An intrigued producer from National Public Radio contacted me about a letter she had recently received describing some fifth graders really trying to help themselves. During our conversation, she described an upcoming program on the nationally syndicated *This American Life* that was dealing with people in difficult situations who would go to incredible lengths to try to solve a problem. As she elaborated, it sounded like a great fit.

NBC news reporter Anna Davlantes with Room 405 students.

Learning from experience, I told her that I was very interested but that I had to relay her proposition to the children, since they would decide whether or not to participate. Although the producer certainly wanted a commitment on the spot, she obliged in consideration of the situation as presented.

The following Monday, I pitched her request to the fifth graders. This time, without hesitation, they agreed to the visit. As they talked about never having been on the radio, they thought this was a great opportunity to spread the word. Several students questioned me as to "what type of radio station we's gonna be on?" Another chimed in, saying, "it probably be on some White station playin' Schultz's bogus elevator music," teasing me about the music I sometimes played in the classroom. Regardless of the ribbing, they were excited about the NPR prospects.

Within days, Ira Glass, host of *This American Life*, and his assistant were at the school armed with a vintage tape recorder and microphone. Before I knew it, a wireless microphone was clipped to my collar. Being recorded for hours would prove to be one of the most uncomfortable things I ever did as a teacher. Everything—each and every word—would be on the record! Cautiously, I tried beginning the day the same way I usually did. Once the bell sounded, the students made their way into the room. Many introduced themselves to our visitors, but others goofed around, waiting for my reaction. This presented a problem, as I wanted, and felt I needed, to appear to be in control so the radio program would capture us at our best. At the same time, I believed I could not exert authority because it would sound as though I was authoritative in my teaching style. Sensing my discomfort, one student persistently tried to get me to respond. He thought it was funny but was aware that I did not.

Following our typical routine, the reporters recorded our every move, and we soon acclimated to the presence of the reporters and their microphones. They focused on group interactions and queried individual children when they felt more clarification was appropriate.

Certain students made sure their voices were heard. Dyneisha made sure they focused on her work as she stayed close to the reporter to give a running commentary. Glass made his way around the room, asking students to highlight the problems. Their graphic descriptions led to a tour of the entire building.

After a full-fledged exploration, it was time to interview me alone. By then, I felt comfortable with their visit and had overcome the initial shock of being recorded for the whole country to hear. My comfort level quickly changed as the interview progressed. Their questions felt loaded, like an interrogation. They asked, "What happens when these kids don't succeed in getting a new school? What is that going to teach them?" I had been wrestling with these issues for some time. I had discussed these topics with friends and colleagues, in addition to discussing it directly with Room 405 students.

Responding with a straightforward, serious demeanor, I explained what I strongly believed about the project's value. I explained that it is not about getting a perfect solution but about the process—learning through active, democratic participation.

When I stressed that the means were at least as important as the potential new school, I got the sense that they were not satisfied. At the time, I felt that they wanted a particular answer regarding the possibility that the project could be miseducative. Amidst their thorough questioning, I reinforced that I did not believe all was lost if the students did not get what they had been working so hard for.

Before leaving the school, the *This American Life* team spent time with the school administrators. After Ira Glass understandably challenged me during his interview of me about the potentially harmful lessons that could emerge from the project, the principal revealed to the radio host his concern that the students might be devalued through the project. Ira Glass quoted the principal saying, "If they don't get what they want," they may believe "that their voice is a small voice and doesn't matter." Although the principal and I differed about this essential aspect, I reconciled myself to it as part of the nature of solving authentic curriculum problems. There were real consequences. My ardent belief was that these were positive experiences that could not be taken away from the students, no matter the outcome of their pursuit.

When the radio show aired during our mid-April spring break, it began with the students' efforts to get a new school and was used to set up the hour-long program titled "Desperate Measures." Throughout the five-minute introduction, the Room 405 students described in detail all the school's problems. The piece included a lot of student voices that led into other segments about people in tough situations where there was no way to come out ahead, no matter what they did. The segment featuring the students focused more on Carr's shameful building than on ways the students were working to solve the identified shortcomings. As I listened to the program, I wondered if my students could come out ahead whether or not the new building was built. In this moment, I began to realize a great opportunity for teaching media literacy to the students after the break.

When the students listened to the NPR program, they liked what they heard. Only one questioned, "Why they spend all that time here and tell so little 'bout us?" I had similar sentiments but was thankful there was no outcry from students about "being treated" or exploited. After all, it was my job to protect them. The student's comment proved to be a good point for discussion and allowed me to remind them that the mass media and representations by it are continually up for analysis, evaluation, and scrutiny.

Glass also captured students describing the school's poor condition. For example, Shaniqua remarked, "Here go a bullet hole in the window. Here go our missing drinking fountain." Malik explained, "We gonna take y'all down to our lunchroom. We got a bootleg lunchroom cause it is a hallway with just tables in it." And Tavon pointed out, "Like our classroom, in the winter the heat was supposed to be on, but we had to put on our hats, our coats, our gloves . . . we can't hardly write because people have on mittens. You know, you can't write with no mittens."

After listening to the piece several times, I decided the story was strong, advocating, and certainly not violating. I did, however, agree with the students that there was so much more that could have been told.

As we discussed how to interpret and make sense of powerful imagery, some students connected to places where the radio story could have been expanded to depict the kids' ways of organizing, working for change, and taking action. Others focused on how there were good reasons to portray the story as it was because of how it captured the listener's attention.

As I was facilitating classroom talk about media literacy, I was personally and privately contemplating whether television and radio were appropriate methods for portraying the students' overall cause. There was certainly the potential for exploitation or misinterpretation of what I saw occurring in our classroom. In the large-group discussion, the consensus of Room 405 was that the publicity was great, but I wanted to make sure it went beyond the surface aspect of Dyneisha's mother's comment about making "my daughter a movie star" or simply getting the students on the airwaves.

We continued our critical analysis in the classroom, and the students made independent decisions about how they viewed the representation in the media. The NPR program undoubtedly got the news out to a much broader, national audience. As a result, the students would soon be approached about being part of a research study focusing on children engaged in curricula that fostered community social action. This additional dimension would again increase their reach, and their story would eventually be integrated into a book being written by a professor from New York City.

5

Process as Product

PRACTICING WHAT I PREACHED

An advocate following the students' campaign e-mailed to inform them that Ralph Nader would be speaking in Chicago. This woman believed that by getting someone famous, such as Nader, on our bandwagon, the project would get more press and ultimately help to achieve the goal. Unfortunately, I had one of the final meetings of a graduate class that conflicted with his speech. I informed the students that my schedule would not allow us to attend.

The class understood that I, too, was a student with responsibilities. Well, everyone except for Reggie understood. Without verbally arguing the point, he nonchalantly put together an information packet containing all of the artifacts of their compelling case: petitions, writing, photos, survey results, and published articles. After assembling the folder, he made a label: "Prepared especially for Mr. Ralph Nader."

Handing me the folder, Reggie said, "It was important to continue makin' people aware of what we doing." As I replied, reiterating my prior commitment, he continued speaking over me. "And, if we really fightin' for what we believe, we can't fight only when it is convenient!"

His persistence was the same mantra I had repeated to the class numerous times before. Reggie, a master at being passive-aggressive, walked away without any further comment. That afternoon, while driving toward the university, I again saw Reggie's specially prepared, canary-yellow folder, this time protruding from my bag. Guilt immediately set in.

The guilt was so deep that I became engrossed in thought about Reggie's comments, my own journal entries, the steadfast advice about having conviction I gave to the children, and pedagogical commitments. I missed the turnoff, subconsciously heading toward the Nader event instead of my graduate class. Although this was my students' fight, didn't I need to practice what I preached? I was just as much a part of the class as any student. I was a role model. I felt obligated to pursue this lead in the same manner I would have expected them to sacrifice something if a similar opportunity was presented.

Because of my late arrival to Nader's talk, I was forced to wait in the lobby. Able to catch only muffled words between cheers from the boisterous audience, I watched "Nader for President" volunteers seeking petition signatures to get Nader on the Illinois ballot.

It struck me that I was there to present Nader with my students' petition as others gathered signatures. Glancing at my watch, knowing I was missing class, I was approached to sign the petition. I did not know what to do. I certainly supported his ballot initiative, as the two-party system clearly was not representing everyone in our country, especially my students. Yet I was concerned that if I signed, others might consider me an activist teacher—pushing a political agenda on my students.

Realizing the hypocrisy of my actions, I feared signing the petition would allow others to assume that I was putting personal beliefs ahead of my students and that my personal convictions were the nexus of their project. Concluding that if I avoided signing and Nader got involved, I would later say, "Nader supported my students, and I did not even sign his petition." Since I was struggling with some of the publicity surrounding the project, and as self-centered as my judgment may sound, I felt the need to protect myself as well as keep my students' efforts clean at every opportunity. And I did not want to be known as the teacher with an agenda pushing political views on students.

Beyond my own pedagogical beliefs, there was something in the back of my mind. Two weeks before, I had received a call from the office of a high-ranking Chicago Public Schools official inquiring about the project. I was shocked by the accusatory nature of this administrator's assistant articulating his point of view on the other end of the line. She attacked me for being behind this since, as she said, there had been too many adults supporting the project and, quite simply, students from the Carr school were not capable of this level of work or self-direction.

Furious about her blatant disregard for my students' abilities, I collected myself before explaining how the efforts evolved out of the Project Citizen curriculum from the Center for Civic Education and the Constitutional Rights Foundation Chicago. As I explained the students' commitment and the action plan they had developed, I emphasized the amazing things they were doing, whether she wanted to believe it or not.

Ignoring my explanation, she interrupted to explain that the official would send a response letter to the fifth graders but that he would not be making an appearance at Carr.

"A letter will not satisfy my students," I said, explaining that Room 405 was demanding a visit. After I clarified the students' request for a personal appearance rather than correspondence, the administrator quickly ended the call, reiterating that someone must be behind this because, as she stated, she got letters all the time from students and these were different and better than any others.

I suppose I was behind this. Wasn't my role as a teacher to support students and encourage learning? My biggest problem was her lack of belief that Carr students were capable of the sophisticated fight. Was it because they were from Cabrini Green? Didn't she think they had it in them? My disgust at the conversation ended in frustration. Not only did the students have their visit request denied, but they never received the promised letter.

It was obvious the phone call had impacted me. I wanted to avoid the label that many had already bestowed on me. Was I an activist? Or was I a teacher who was supporting and nurturing the learners in my classroom? Was there a difference? And why had detractors framed being an activist so negatively?

After waiting for over an hour at the Nader event, I was finally permitted to enter the auditorium. As the audience flowed toward the exits, I sought out a person in charge and asked him to give the folder to Nader on behalf of the Room 405 fifth graders. He asked, "Why don't you give it to him yourself?" and grabbed me by the shirtsleeve, leading me through a series of checkpoints and back rooms to the area where Nader would be answering media questions.

The chance to actually give the documents to Nader himself and potentially speak with him about my students' work was surreal. While waiting in the press room, I talked with several journalists and reporters also awaiting his arrival. The classroom's journey was hard to resist. They, too, became interested in the students' achievements and inquired about arranging visits.

People were shocked that fifth graders from the inner city were willing and able to do something good for themselves by taking on a project with such dedication. Some of these reactions were belittling and offensive, but it was an opportunity to change their viewpoints by spreading awareness of the smart young citizens' capability, regardless of their neighborhood.

All the waiting paid off. When Nader entered the room, the gentleman who had gotten me through security pushed me forward, introducing me to Nader. "This schoolteacher has something to share with you," he said.

Not knowing how long I would have Nader's attention, I nervously gave my best sales pitch. After listening to me ramble for about 10 seconds, Nader interjected, "Your high school students are doing some amazing work!"

As the television, radio, and newspaper reporters shoved tape recorders in my face, I emphatically corrected him. "No, no. This is the work of a group of fifth graders from Cabrini Green." Awed by the work presented, Nader examined each page of the packet. He pledged to write about our project.

Just 72 hours later, my phone rang. "Brian, Ralph Nader here."

I could hardly believe that Ralph Nader was calling me. He was overwhelmed by the fifth graders' work and wanted to continue learning about their project. He fired question after question during the half-hour conversation. Comfortably answering his queries about how the project had evolved, I also shared my views regarding teaching and learning.

It would not be long before Nader delivered as promised. The article would have tremendous traction when it appeared on his Web site and that of the popular progressive news clearinghouse Common Dreams. The essay, "Fifth-grade Students at a Crumbling Chicago Elementary School Challenge Political Indifference" (Nader, 2004a), appropriately portrayed the students' fight juxtaposed against the current, distorted U.S. educational policy.

"Mr. Schultz, what have you done now?" my principal asked when I walked into the school the day Nader's article was published. Unbeknownst to me, the published article had included the principal's e-mail address. "There must be thousands of e-mails," he explained. The deluge of commendation for his support for students was remarkable. Not sure at first if he was enthusiastic or annoyed by the attention, he calmed my anxiety by telling me that he had already responded to dozens and it was only eight o'clock in the morning.

The Nader article was accurate and informative. Nader (2004a) introduced the Room 405 curriculum by putting it in context:

> Carr Community Academy is a crumbling elementary school in Chicago next to one of the largest and most perilous public housing projects—Cabrini Green. It also is the location of one of the more spectacular fifth-grade classes in the country.
>
> In Room 405, since December, the entire course curriculum is devoted to one project and one goal—document the terrible disrepair and lack of facilities of the school and build community, state and national support for a new school! (online)

Nader continued, describing the project's strategy and accomplishments:

> The youngsters appear transformed. Their attendance rate is 98 percent and coming from a part of Chicago rife with drugs, street violence, gang activity, physical deterioration and unemployment, this is testimony to their interest. They design each part of their research and action strategy. . . .
>
> Interviews, video documentary, expository writing, letters/emails, direct action, surveys, petitions, news releases, photography fundraising and research. They're into the costs for the new school, where the money has to come from, the position of the Board of Education (distant), the response from the elected officials (mostly cool up to now) and how to get media for their cause (they have been interviewed by the *Chicago Tribune* and NPR, among several news outlets).
>
> Their self-confidence and maturity are growing. They sense that they have started a process of change. (Nader, 2004a, online)

Not only did this article praise their work; they were touted as "one of the more spectacular fifth-grade classes in the country!" (Nader, 2004a). Nader's succinct chronicle of Project Citizen brought a broad range of support. Numerous suggestions, ideas, and communiqués resulted from his article. People from all over the world responded with praise, encouragement, and additional references for the students to read.

As it would turn out, Nader continued to stay in touch with the Carr fifth graders. Eventually, he would feature them in his book *The Good Fight* (2004b) as well as take time away from his presidential campaign to pay a visit, complimenting their grassroots efforts for change.

DO YOU HAVE ANY PETS?

Visitors to our classroom became commonplace. They came to be interviewed as guest speakers, from the media, or simply as interested observers. They were equipped with video cameras, tape recorders, or notepads, ready to learn why these young citizens were so enamored with their school project.

Celia Oyler, a professor at Teachers College, Columbia University, visited the class for an entire week. She sought to incorporate the students' project into a book that she was writing.

The students arranged action-packed days during her visit. Tyrone noted, "This lady is different 'cause she actually be spending time with us . . . a whole week. I think that gonna help her know us better so she can tell others."

The students wanted Oyler to have plenty of data collection and observation opportunities, as her purpose in their classroom was to gain insight on how a classroom curriculum can be based on social action. Each day of her visit had at least one special thing for her to see.

Because Oyler's presence was nonthreatening, students warmed up to her quickly. Almost immediately, she was included as part of the class. After a rapport-building day, the students eagerly showed off their work, taking time to talk with Celia individually and in separate focus groups. Several children even took her home so she could talk with their parents. In her thank-you letter to the class after her visit, Oyler applauded Room 405, comparing them to other classrooms she observed:

> You were by far the youngest students attempting to change something and secondly, you have done way more outreach and publicity. . . . How amazing is that? The youngest students accomplishing the most sophisticated project!"

Oyler also stressed how "polite and welcoming" the students were. Then she emphasized their learning:

> The other thing I wanted to make sure you are aware of is how much your academic skills are being strengthened by the project. . . . When you look back on 5th grade I want to make sure you realize how much math and reading and writing and social studies you learned without even knowing it.
>
> But I guess the most important things you learned are the things you are already aware of. You learned that people when they work together can analyze a problem and come up with a solution. You've learned to find out who the key decision makers are about any issue and contact them directly for more information. You learned how to inform other people about the problem and the solution and organize for your issue. You learned how to persuade people with facts (and how to gather the facts that would persuade them!).
>
> In almost all my interviews I found out that your class of 5th graders learned that you can work to make this world a better place.

When we spoke before her visit, Celia conveyed to me that the students' campaign was perfect to feature in her upcoming book. She asked if she could observe and interact with students, administrators, and parents. Knowing that the students needed to have input on big decisions, I encouraged the professor to reach out to the class via e-mail so they could make the final determination.

Within an hour, an e-mail appeared in the students' inbox. Oyler's message explained her project and how she had heard about the students (via NPR). Detailing her curiosity about their work, she asked to be their guest.

By now, accustomed to screening potential visitors, Demetrius and Artell sprang into action. They wrote back, questioning Celia prior to accepting her solicitation. The questions were specific concerning how she was going to feature Room 405 in her book. Their curiosities allowed me to sit back and observe as they created an interrogation based on their agenda:

> Why do you want to write about us?
> What are you going to say about us in your book?
> Who is going to read this book when it's finished?

They wanted to know about Celia as a person, not just about her interest in them. Demetrius said to Artell, "If she's comin' here to find out 'bout us, we needs to check her first." With his matter-of-fact statement, they continued their list:

Have you been to Chicago before?
What about Cabrini Green?
When you come to Chicago, where are you going to stay?
What should we call you?
Do you have any pets? If so, what kind?

I wondered where on earth they had come up with that last question. As funny as this question appeared to me, these two students were genuine in asking. The letter closed, "When we hear back from you about these questions, the class will vote to decide if you should come." Signing it, "Happy you are interested in us fifth graders," they sent it off.

I waited until the e-mail was sent before asking how and why they came up with the questions. They explained that they wanted to know how Carr would appear in the book and would only accept her if "we lookin' good."

When asked about the pet question, both looked dumbfounded, as if I was foolish for even asking. Artell explained, "We figure if she likes animals and gots pets, she'll be a nice lady to us. It's gonna be our test."

As faulty as their logic may have seemed to me, it was sincere, and they appeared genuinely interested. How could I argue with their test? The students had found value in setting parameters for who was allowed to visit our room.

Celia provided serious responses to each question within hours. The boys were able to share her answers with the class for a vote the same day. And yes, apparently, she was quite fond of cats. Unanimously, the class voted to allow Celia to observe their class for a week in May. The class enjoyed her responses, believing she was a good person, and were eager to have a book written about them.

Although the students' screening of Celia might seem like a cute story of kids using pet caretaking as their litmus test for determining classroom access, it is much more than that. The permission given to the students to make key critical decisions—including classroom gatekeeping—was evolving over time. The students developed scrutinizing rationales and were demonstrating their savvy to screen visitors. In late May, Celia arrived at Carr.

The students' response to another article written about their pursuit was one of Celia's first observations. They had communicated, via e-mail, with Marion Brady, a retired educator turned newspaper columnist in Orlando, Florida. Brady, a well-known author in curriculum circles for his splendid, inspirational books on integrated curriculum, unfortunately was not, as one student suggested, able to bring the students down to Orlando for an interview.

Their response to his writing dealt with a continuing classroom discussion about how one's perspective determines the meaning of a statement, incident, or other interaction. Sometimes, I had explained, you look at the literal meaning, while at other moments you delve into the idiosyncrasies of the source or situation. When we would deconstruct texts, the interpretation was in the eyes of the beholder.

Such was the case with Brady's essay in the *Orlando Sentinel*. Comparing our classroom to the current state of affairs in American education in a way similar to Nader's piece, the article began, "At a time when many educators, usually under duress, have turned their classrooms into mind-numbing, joy-killing, drill-them-'til-they-drop test-prep factories, Schultz has taken a different approach" (Brady, 2004, p. A19). As it continued, detailing how we approached the different school subjects, the author provided one perspective of the school's neighborhood:

> Room 405 of the Carr Community Academy . . . smack up against Cabrini Green, the public-housing project with a national reputation for gang activity, drugs, street violence, unemployment and dysfunctional families. Cabrini Green has all the stuff of which failure is made, and it often delivers door-to-door. (p. A19)

I interrupted the choral reading to emphatically repeat the statement, "Cabrini Green has all the stuff of which failure is made, and it often delivers door-to-door."

"What does this mean exactly?" I asked.

After a pause, Demetrius offered his literal interpretation of this line. I was fishing for a deeper answer, but Demetrius and the rest of his classmates were not interested in taking the bait.

I hoped to get the students fired up because an outsider was critiquing their neighborhood. With Celia present, I wanted to reignite discussion about perspective, building on previous classroom talk about people unaware of particulars who make assumptions to characterize situations.

Was the neighborhood as bad as people depicted? To me, it felt peculiar that in every article written about the students' project, the author always felt a need to paint the bleakest picture. Did the article really uplift the students, or did it perpetuate the stereotypes? Was the author truly highlighting how spectacular their classroom situation was without even visiting the school? On one hand, it bothered me to read an outsider's negative comments on the neighborhood—not that I was an insider myself. But on the other, this was an avenue for the students' story to be told and voices heard, and the author, in this case, was a champion for their cause.

Portraying the community with a hopeless undertone by describing people and families who don't care was contrary to the reality I had observed, and, therefore, I wanted to engage my students in this conversation. The students were not interested in discussing issues of race or class, but rather analyzed the author's writing line by line. We proceeded until we reached a section that addressed the reasons the author believed the classroom was a success.

Although the author detailed four reasons, the students simply could not get past the first: "What brings the kids to class? Without a doubt, reason No. 1 is Brian Schultz. He's demonstrating the impossible-to-measure impact of a teacher who cares about, listens to, and genuinely respects kids" (Brady, 2004, p. A19).

This provided the opportunity for them to take a jab at me. The article conveniently praised me as the number-one reason for their success. Demetrius, now fired up and egged on by a chorus of his peers' chuckles and boos, shouted, "How bogus you be number one! We should be number one. We doing everything 'round here."

Demetrius and the others were right. They were the ones who were doing all of the work, and they should be recognized for it. Although Demetrius challenged the first reason, believing the author erroneously gave me credit for the project, he found solace in the insight of the remaining three reasons,

> Two: One of the most powerful human needs is for autonomy, independence, [and] control over one's actions. . . . Within the narrow boundaries that our traditional approach to school permits, Schultz's fifth graders have autonomy and control.

> Three: The kids are out of their seats, dealing with the real world in all its intellectually stimulating complexity. Contrast that with the "sit down, shut up, listen-because-you'll-need-to-know-this-next-year" fare they'd come to expect.

Four: Succeed or fail, what they're trying to do is genuinely important, not merely in the context of schooling, but in the larger world beyond the fence. It's not just about getting ready for the next grade, not just a game or simulation, not just preparing for a test, not just jumping through yet another ritual hoop. . . . It's learning as means to end—making Cabrini Green a better place.

(Brady, 2004, p. A19)

Although this discussion did not employ the same critical lens used when we read from Kozol's *Savage Inequalities*, the neighborhood portrayal was apparently not interesting to them. I learned that students could deconstruct text with a decisive eye, but only when they were self-motivated, not when provoked. Whether the presence of a visitor inhibited them or the issue did not bother them like it bothered me is not the point. I was taught by students to let my leading question go and move on. It was important to let the students lead the whole discussion here, even if they may have left out issues that seemed important to me. The deliberation was lively. The students were engaged. If I stepped in and took control, the shared classroom authority would have been squelched, and perhaps in the future the class might not have been as willing to actively deliberate about their viewpoints or opinions.

The week continued with a visit by a video editor and producer, Mitchell, or as the students called him, "The DVD guy with d'funky threads." Weeks before, the students had decided that producing a DVD would be a good way to extend their triumphs and put everything together. Mitch was there to show them how to create their entire production. Even though most artifacts were already published on their Web site, no students had home Internet access. Each did, however, have a DVD player at home. The DVD production was a great alternative for the students to view the extensive list of news and radio programming, video documentaries, and even the articles written about them. With Mitch's guidance and expertise, the students designed the DVD not only to include the video and sound but also to house and make accessible all of the written artifacts through an interactive menu. Instead of just creating the DVD for them, Mitch insisted they be a part of the development. With the students' great feedback, the DVD project demonstrated their willingness to explore different ways of sharing their ideas.

During Celia's visit, the students also prepared for their Project Citizen hearing, which was scheduled to take place the following week. As part of the Project Citizen curriculum, the Constitutional Rights Foundation Chicago held forums where students presented their public policy class projects in front of a panel of experts and other students. The students rehearsed speeches and created final touches for their presentation in an effort to guarantee proper presentation in front of an audience.

The entire week had been filled with an intensity that offered Celia a candid view of our classroom. The students benefited from this prolonged visit as they inquired and learned from the guest, too. Valuing Celia's opinion, they believed she really helped their cause. Their original queries and her responses were indeed good indicators.

THE BESTEST YEAR EVER

As the Greyhound Bus rolled back into Chicago the first Thursday in June, the Room 405 students reminisced about their experiences on an invited trip to the Illinois State Board of Education (ISBE) in the state capital. An ISBE technology director wanted our class to be featured on a Webcast after seeing the opportunity to promote technology infusion in all subjects via a student perspective—something that had not been done before. Despite the fact that the curriculum highlighted the state's glaring educational funding shortfalls, he concluded that the students' social justice fight and candid confrontation with inequities through the tech-rich project, notably the kid-produced DVD and Web site, would be a perfect way to encourage other teachers and students.

Ironically, the trip's funding was secured through the Chicago Public Schools. Although the highest-level decision makers at the board of education chose not to respond to the students' relentless phone calls, letters, and e-mails, other board employees took notice, securing funds to pay the trip expenses.

The students planned the entire trip. They made contact with the legislators who had visited their classroom to schedule meetings in Springfield. Malik's goal was "a pimped-out royal treatment," so he worked hard to make the proper arrangements. The students announced their upcoming visit on their Web site, bragging that they were the only students in the state to have this honor!

Quite proud of this distinction, and thankful for the opportunity, Room 405 students took the first bus headed to Springfield so they could arrive early for an action-packed day. For several, it was their first time outside Chicago.

Thumbing through magazines, playing games, and snapping photos on disposable cameras throughout the bus ride, the students casually discussed how they were going to present Project Citizen on the Webcast. Finally, after stops at several points of interest, we arrived at the Illinois State Board of Education offices. Wasting no time, the technology director quickly ushered the class into a high-tech television studio and gave them the floor.

Embracing the opportunity, Shaniqua spoke first: "This has been my favorite year in school. We do really fun things every day, like finding ways to get a better school. Our teacher really wants us to do well, but we get to figure it all out on our own."

Tavon agreed with his classmate: "We really like every day 'cause we gets to do cool things. Things other kids never do, like shooting video or building Web sites."

As if performing a script he had rehearsed for weeks, Malik continued:

You see, our school is pretty bad, messed up. The building be all broke. It ain't no place to learn. But this year has been the bestest year ever. We always got guests coming to talk to us. And we do things other kids our age don't get to do. . . . We trying to get a new school for the community and this technology helps kids learn and grow and get stuff done—check out all we've done.

After taking a breath, he added, "If you don't do Project Citizen, you should!"

We've Got Soap!

On their Web site, the students tracked the various school improvements that had begun to occur. They also documented the additional media coverage about their fight. According to an article in *Education Week*, "Sidewalks outside the building were repaired. Water fountains inside began to work. New light bulbs suddenly brightened classrooms" (Gewertz, 2004, p. 10).

My journal showed both my excitement and my disgust: "Workers were fixing sinks, the telephone lines, and the building's doors, but I could not believe how pitiful it was watching third graders running down the hall with hands lathered up, shouting 'we've got soap, we've got soap.'" Despite these physical changes, there was still no direct response from city or school board officials regarding the students' requests.

As Carr got a much-needed facelift, the class was paid a visit by the building engineer. Although he rarely came into classrooms to interact with students, the engineer had an important announcement. Standing in the front of Room 405, he told them that the windows at Carr Academy were all going to be replaced! The engineer explained that he and the principal had been asking the board to fix the horrible, foggy windows for years but nobody had listened. As he continued with his praise, the engineer said that because the students had demanded changes, the people downtown had listened. He said that he was, and they should be, very proud of all their class was doing for the school.

Milestones, Honors, and Achievement

The perpetually foggy windows of aged, bulletproof Plexiglas—the hallmark of Carr's façade—were to be history.

Dissatisfied with superficial results, the students continued their quest for their perfect solution, a groundbreaking for a new school building. Complete with poster boards and pamphlets, the class presented a compelling case at the board's June capital improvement hearing detailing the building's gross inadequacies. They went beyond simply learning about the functions of governments. Through their active civic participation, they clearly articulated to the capital improvement officers where the board's system had broken down. Room 405 had become expert in being active democratic participants. In so doing they were also recognized with awards, honors, and distinctions locally and nationally.

The Northwestern University Collaboratory Project honored the students with the Project of the Year Award. The Center for Civic Education highlighted their efforts on their Web site as the most influential Project Citizen class. The Constitutional Rights Foundation Chicago bestowed both the Most Creative Project Award and Young Citizen Activists Award on them, and they received recognition from the Illinois State Board of Education. The students took great pride in these awards and made certain that every visitor saw their multitude of plaques, certificates, and trophies. In addition to the awards, Room 405 was asked to keynote the Center for Civic Education's National Conference on Project Citizen.

Beyond the awards and honors collected by the children, there were quantitative facts and statistics demonstrating the project's success. The students boasted an unprecedented 98% attendance rate. As the class included several chronic truants from the previous year, this was certainly a tremendous accomplishment.

Achievement was also demonstrated in the students' standardized test performance. Though I advocate against standardized testing and the hyper-accountability shackling the American educational system, this achievement is worthy of note. Although Room 405 students were forced to use outdated resources and take standardized tests amid unseasonably high temperatures in an un-air-conditioned classroom, they proved successful even on measures that were stacked against them from the start.

When questioned about their results on these tests, I tend to avoid directly answering because I do not want to reduce the classroom and its glory to a biased achievement test. If pressed, however, I happily divulge that students' scores improved significantly over the year. This was not to say each student scored higher than the previous year, but 35% of those who had not reached the national norm for the Iowa Test of Basic Skills the previous year made it to this important milestone. This significant student achievement (albeit on a poorly designed and improperly used indicator) cannot be overlooked.

Although I cannot prove that our curriculum affected their achievement, allowing students to co-create a curriculum centered around what was important to them produced significant results. Apparently, those Carr students *were* capable of doing amazing things!

School's Out Forever

> As part of our overall commitment to improve the Chicago Public Schools, each year we consider whether to open new schools and close others. The decision to close any school is a difficult one because all schools are anchors to their communities and treasures to families and alumni. . . . I am proposing to recommend to the Board of Education . . . that a number of schools be closed at the end of the current year. (Chicago Public Schools, 2004, online)

After thousands of dollars were spent on costly improvements, and with more expensive renovations scheduled, this statement by the Chicago schools' superintendent to Carr faculty had not been anticipated. Although the entire school community knew that closing Carr was always possible, no one could believe the reality when it hit.

All the writing about alternatives, including a potential school closure, could not have prepared us for the news. I wrote in my journal: "Immediately tears flowed. . . . What a blend of emotions, tremendous shock at first, but then almost immediately the anger came. How could the Board of Education have ignored my students when they knew this announcement was imminent?"

With a flurry of questions running through my head, I considered the entire profession and my role in it: "Do I want to teach anymore?" I wondered. "Do I care anymore? Was this all worth it?" I couldn't believe what was going on around me. I felt like I was at a funeral—the death of Carr—and I was scared.

We had discussed this possibility at great length in the classroom. The students had been determined to fight for their cause, despite knowing that the chance of successfully saving Carr was small. But how was I going to break the news to my fifth graders? As I made my way to the classroom that morning, I somehow pulled myself together to tell Room 405 the news that would break their hearts. Following my announcement, the classroom was in a frenzy. There were celebratory shouts and fearful crying. Considering their wide range of emotions, the teacher in me encouraged them to respond to the news in their journals.

Amazingly, many were able to separate their disappointment from the value of their campaign. They were certainly more resilient than I was, and their fortitude was reflected in their journal entries. The fifth graders initially reacted with sentiments of frustration and being "very, very upset" and "feelin' like we wasted our breath."

"We did all this work and now they are shutting the school down?"

"I think it not fair, I feel bad beacuse we have been working on project citizen for six months and that is a long time for 5 graders. So did we do this project for nothing?"

But through the disappointment, the students showed continued bravery and were able to see the value of the experience.

"We have got heard by a lot of people like being on the newspaper and the television . . . we were a good group of kids fighting for what is right. Carr has Carr pride, and I will keep it when I go to a different school."

"We did not do this work for nothing we did it because we wanted to."

"That must mean that it is time for us to go to more big and better things."

"This made me feel good and proud."

"We did get some accompioshments."

"I beivleve that i will be able to use the skill in the future becuase we learned how the government works."

They also saw value in the project itself: "Project Citizen is a real good project because it helps you with different problems that you might want to fix in you community."

"I learned alot this year . . . I think that this is a good project because kids get to do things that others dont."

"I think other classes shoudl do it."

"It gets me to stay focused."

"You don't never have to give up because they say you won't get your goal."

"Project citizen let us do things we normally would not do. in the future I can do these things again. project citizen taught me a lot."

"I think other kids would enjoy doing this kidn of project cuase it lasts long."

"I will remember it as a good thing even we did not get a new school. i would recommend another school doing project citizen."

The students were not the only ones reacting to the devastating news. Many supporters responded, inquiring about student reaction to the announcement.

Who's Responsible?

I had a lot to think about as well. Over the next couple of days, I wrestled with reflections on what had occurred and whether, in fact, my students and I were responsible for the closure. My journal overflowed with entries about all my feelings. I wrote:

> On Sunday, I broke down. I think it was a combination of dealing with the students and the staff getting so screwed. This faculty is unlike any other group of teachers. They are amazing people. They come into Cabrini Green, many of whom could teach anywhere, and have been doing it for so long proves their dedication and devotion to children in an underserved and disadvantaged neighborhood. These teachers treat the students as their own. They do not deserve this.
>
> I cried myself to sleep thinking that these kids get the shaft in so many ways. I know the kids can do whatever it takes, but I feel like the social engineering by the city and school board, along with society's acceptance of the inequalities put these children in a precarious situation. Were they not meant to achieve? Try telling them that!

Much of my own anger turned into guilt. Several Carr staff pointed to Room 405, Project Citizen, and me as the cause of the school closing. Did we cause this to happen? Or were we scapegoats?

As I wondered about the outcomes, I discussed my concerns with several close colleagues. I was particularly interested in their take on Carr's closing. They clarified their reasons for teaching, and in hearing this I was able to see why there was much value in Room 405's pursuits.

They explained that teaching is an opportunity to share an experience, to influence, and to nurture. They also clarified that the students in Room 405 may very well have influenced the board's decision but added that no one should ever take away this most significant learning experience and opportunity for these students. "If you are any kind of ethical teacher," one said, "you have an obligation to nurture this kind of learning, even when the stakes are high and the consequences severe."

Despite the devastating announcement, the students demonstrated their perseverance by continuing to work in line with their beliefs. They reflected a firm commitment to their cause, no matter the outcome.

After reading each child's journal entry, I wondered whether the sentiments were genuine. Did they feel the need to write positively about the project because they believed that's what was expected? Did the students really believe Project Citizen was the positive endeavor they described? Did these young activists believe others should have the Project Citizen experience they advocated? Were they truly sincere about their frustration, yet hopeful about their futures?

Once back in Room 405, after my difficult weekend wrestling with the news, I realized the admirable truthfulness of the statements based on their attitudes and willingness to continue finding different avenues of persevering. Intent on keeping the project going during the final weeks of school, the students displayed their ongoing dedication. They continued to interact with their contacts and tied up loose ends, while also establishing new lines of investigation. Impressed by the resolve of the students, I watched them as they tried to understand the predicament in which we found ourselves. And even though they realized they were not going to achieve their perfect solution, they stuck to their commitments and reflected on all of their accomplishments.

Using the same skills refined throughout the previous months, Room 405 focused on the school board's decision to shut Carr Academy. They wanted to determine whether their efforts were actually responsible for the school's demise.

Their examination showed they were interested not only in the product or end results but also in the process. They readily transferred skills from one mode of the project to another. It was not always about winning or achieving the goal, but about what occurred during the struggle. They really had become critical examiners and challengers of the status quo. The project was a success.

After telephone calls and examinations of recent Web site postings about school closings in Chicago, the students continued investigating. Amid further research, the students made an incredible finding. The school board had actually made its decision to close Carr long before Room 405 even began its Project Citizen efforts. They uncovered a previously undisclosed document on the same Web site where they had found information about the slated new school building months earlier. A decision, made almost two years earlier, indicated that Carr Academy would likely be shut down.

"They knew before we started that they be closing us down," Artell sullenly told his peers when he found the information on the Internet.

Cabrini Green in its current state as a housing project, the students found out, was not part of Chicago's plan for urban renewal. The promised new school had been tabled long before the fifth graders embarked on their pursuit. In addition to the board of education document, they found an article in the *Chicago Reader* reporting that a contributing factor in Carr's closure had to do with real estate developers getting access to the valuable land the school was on. Although the details found in the article were not surprising to the students, it was important that others were documenting what they suspected.

As the students discovered articles critiquing the Board of Education's decision in newspapers and on Web sites, they were assured that the decision was about money, not about education or their intervention. Their findings pointed to the fact that Carr's land was extremely valuable to the city. According to the article in the *Chicago Reader*, the students were even cited as trying to do something about it:

> Once again schools CEO [name removed] wants to close schools in poor, black neighborhoods. . . . About seven years ago [the Chief Executive Officer of Chicago Public Schools] promised the community that the city would build a new Carr . . . but construction on a new Carr never started. . . . Locals now believe they were suckered. . . . Earlier this year, fifth-grade students . . . put together a Web site on which they pressed the board to make good on the

promise to build a new school. . . . This is not about education. This is about getting access to property. (Joravsky, 2004, p. 5)

As the Chicago Housing Authority tore down students' residences and families were forced out of their homes, no new students came to Carr in its last year, despite the school board's busing policy. Unfortunately, this information was made public only after the school-closing announcement. Nevertheless, through a school administrator, the students identified a change to the district's busing policy for bringing additional students to Carr. This decision inevitably controlled enrollment, which forced the school to close at the end of the year. Room 405 revealed that the school board was the real culprit—not them.

Again, these savvy researchers exposed the truth about their situation, proving to fingerpointers (and themselves) that they were not to blame. With the guilt off their conscience, they were able to focus on the multitude of "wins" that had occurred throughout the year. They had reasons to celebrate even though this was not the victory they had strived for all year long.

NADER COMES TO CARR

While the students were performing their detective work, they prepared for a Saturday visit by Ralph Nader. With only one week left in the school year, the students were determined to keep this commitment. They maintained an interest in sharing their experiences and were still eager to come in on their days off to demonstrate their dedication to the cause of getting better schools for their community.

Using the same polished speeches they had used for their Project Citizen hearing, the students took center stage, in Carr's foyer, to present all of their work. Nader sat beside the students in the audience, among the numerous television, radio, and newspaper reporters as well as Carr teachers. The students were the guests of honor, and they took the lead. They were the reason for Nader's visit, and it was important to keep them in the spotlight. The students made their presentation to Nader and the audience gathered in the Carr hallway for over an hour. They detailed the evolution of their project and all they had accomplished.

After the students highlighted the curriculum through well-rehearsed speeches, I made my way up to address the group before introducing

Ralph Nader visits Carr Community Academy.

Nader. Standing before all my students, a sense of pride overwhelmed me. Choked up, and with tears welling in my eyes, I briefly described how this project and the students' emergent efforts to solve a problem important to them made our learning come alive.

After my brief introduction, Nader took the stage in Carr's makeshift auditorium. His message to the students was a great culmination to a year of tremendous work:

> I read about what the students were doing. Of course, for many years, I have believed that to learn reading, writing, or arithmetic is done indirectly, not directly. Because by focusing on a problem that the students really care about, then the students really get excited. Then they learn all kinds of things they would not ordinarily have learned. They are motivated to, in this case, document how deteriorating their school is and their demand for a new school. And, in so doing, look what they are doing.
>
> First of all, they are learning how to assemble facts from observation, from reading, and from interviewing. That is a pretty important way to learn. Second, they are learning how to make some sense out of the facts: working on the computer, designing the data, writing letters to aldermen, writing letters to people in Washington, learning that it is their right to have a good school that is safe, that is well equipped, and that services their educational needs. . . .

So I am reading all of these materials that your teacher gave me. And I am saying look at all the work that has been done about how to teach students, how do you motivate them to learn. All the studies and conferences and books that have been written and theories, and what it really comes down to is your teacher asked you: What do you want to study? . . .

This is a very important class, a very important project that you are engaged in. . . . You ought to be proud of yourselves. I understand your concentration on your work has been sky-high. Your attendance has been sky-high. Your attention span is expanding. Your vocabulary is expanding. Your ability to do pie charts and those things that you do with the computer is expanding, and your knowledge of the world at large is expanding because your school relates to the board of education, the board of education relates to the aldermen and relates to the mayor. It relates to the city. . . . You are learning all these things way beyond reading, writing, and arithmetic. So I hope this idea that you are making work with your teacher, Brian Schultz, will spread to other schools and others classes. (Nader, 2004c)

Following his address, Nader interacted with the audience. One notable question from a student focused on continuing to fight even if the odds may be against you. Nader promptly responded,

There is an old phrase that says the only place that democracy comes before work is in the dictionary. You know that if you are playing sports and you are behind the other team, you don't give up. So if you are playing basketball in the third quarter and you are behind 15 or 20 points, you don't go up to the coach and say let's call it a day when you are learning something and you are trying to change something. Like you are trying to get a new school, not only for you but for the students that come after you. . . .

For a lot of reasons, you should never give up. Once the other side thinks you are going to give up, the other side is going to put the pressure on you. . . . You really find out a lot about yourself when you are in a fight like this. . . .

You always have to persevere. Learn what it took to win the civil rights laws, overcome slavery . . . all of that took people who don't give up; pressing, pressing, pressing. That is what you do when you play sports. That's what you do when you are engaged in citizen action.

So this project that you have is teaching you all sorts of things that you cannot put a number on, like a test number. These standardized tests do not test your intelligence, your many intelligences. It is developing character. It is developing resilience. After a while, that spells self-confidence. Once you have self-confidence, everything starts falling into place. (Nader, 2004c)

As students continued the questions, some showed Nader their DVD and Web site as they discussed Carr's imminent closing. They were eager to bring up their Carr pride; show off their many awards; discuss how school was about the people inside the building, not the building itself; and talk about Cabrini's gentrification. As they continued in conversation with Nader, he asked why so many people were interested in their story. Dyneisha snapped: "People think a bunch of Black kids from Cabrini Green could not do this, but we showed them and everyone else. Everyone needs a good place to learn and all them others is feeling our pain!"

As Nader finished his talking points, he said, "Just think, you are only in the fifth grade now. What are you going to do next year? . . . Imagine what you are going to be able to do when you are in the sixth grade, the seventh grade." As Nader continued with accolades, he said, as he sat beside the students while watching their video documentary, "This is really amazing. I cannot tell you how impressed I am. It is really magnificent! It should be shown all around the country" (Nader, 2004c).

BITTERSWEET FINAL DAYS

Only one week of school, and one week before the closing of Carr Academy, remained after Nader's Saturday visit. This end-of-year routine had finality. Just as the *Chicago Tribune* had reported months earlier, Carr's operation would be combined with the Cresswell school. Students would transfer. Neighborhood attendance boundaries would expand. Carr teachers and administrators would follow the students to the new school based on need.

These final days were bittersweet. Although still grieving about the irrevocable decision made for us, the students and I spent time recollecting and reminiscing about our foray into city and school politics. As we talked about what could have been, we also shared stories about our remarkable accomplishments.

As we packed up the room, there was an eerie feeling to it. At the same time, there was fresh hope in the realization that the students were fully aware of their capabilities, with their limitless futures ahead of them. None of us were quite certain where those futures would take them, but we were united in knowing that spectacular things really could happen along the way.

The last day at Carr was the end of an era, but amidst its finality, hopefulness was palpable. The students' journal entries on Carr's last day demonstrated their positive spirit despite the disappointing situation. Tyrone wrote, "This is just the beginning. I am going to be somebody, and I am never going to give up." The entries of others had a similar tone and optimism. Undoubtedly, a distinct Carr pride would follow the Room 405 students to their new school and beyond.

In his follow-up article on the students' resolve, the headline of the *Chicago Tribune*'s Eric Zorn (2004b) read: "Pupils' Battle a Success" (p. B1). In addition to Zorn, other journalists praised the project outcomes. And, as an article in *Education Week* aptly quoted the students,

> "I'm a little bit mad," 5th grader Tavon wrote in his journal when he learned the school might close. "We have done all this work . . . but even though we are not getting a new school, we have done great things." (Gewertz, 2004, p. 10)

Great things indeed!

6

Justice-Oriented Teaching

Photo: Phyllis Burstein

NEGOTIATING RISKS

Should teachers have agendas? Whose agenda should it be? When teachers challenge the dominant culture of measurement, standards, and curriculum mandated by federal, state, and local governments as well as school boards to enhance student learning, they may be alienated or pejoratively labeled "maverick" or even "radical." Where can teachers seeking to engage their classrooms in democratic practice get support? Should they be able to follow their visions, even if they are in conflict with current reform efforts? How teachers are viewed in their respective schools and communities raises questions about the idea of whether a teacher should be an activist, someone who takes direct action to achieve a social or political goal, or advocate, one who speaks or writes in support or defense of a group or cause.

Teachers are usually seen as selfless people who have dedicated themselves to helping and nurturing young people. However, this generosity is often questioned when teachers seek to make their classrooms justice-oriented. Teaching is not an ideologically neutral practice, and although I felt that being an activist would be interpreted as forcing my politics on my students, it is imperative that the teacher be political, especially in the current state of affairs, in which one-size-fits-all testing is prescribed as the only way to improve education. While I may have been aware of my status as an activist teacher, I struggled with this label. If I identified with this label, why was this a constant struggle for me? What does it take for teachers to reconcile the interests of their students, their ethical and moral obligations as educators, and the notion of not "rocking the boat" in today's educational and political climate?

Teachers teaching for social justice maintain a curricular stance rooted in and relevant to the lives of students. With a focus on critical, multicultural, antiracist, and antioppressive perspectives, teachers focus on meaningful hands-on, experiential, and participatory activities that seek to help students (and themselves) to critically think about social, political, and economic problems. Teachers and students learn alongside one another in culturally sensitive and culturally relevant spaces. Academic rigor is paramount because curriculum delivered within a social justice context has a tendency to move beyond the school structure (see Ayers, Hunt, & Quinn, 1998; Bigelow, Christensen, Karp, Miner, & Peterson, 1994; Kumashiro, 2002).

In justice-oriented classrooms, the risks for teachers and students potentially multiply. Teachers who teach against the norms and allow their classroom curricula to become integrated and based on the students' priority concerns may unwittingly put themselves into the line of fire. Teachers who permit their classrooms to be driven by the students must understand that they may be challenged by other teachers and by the administration of their school or district. At Carr, I felt that I had a moral obligation to allow students a stake in the curricular decision making of the classroom and, therefore, was willing to face critique and criticism. Other teachers interested in creating this sort of classroom should be aware of the potential risks and finger-pointing that may result.

In many ways, this fight for what the students believed to be right totally aligned with my personal beliefs or "agenda." I needed to be the advocate for my students, with their best interest as my ultimate goal. As a teacher interested in providing this type of classroom opportunity, I knew that my students needed space to deliberate and take responsibility for their actions—even if the consequences were not what I wanted. This also meant that I might confront accusations, reprimands, or even job termination for maintaining this social justice stance. I had to be prepared for challenges from teachers, administrators, parents, and students who were not used to maintaining an approach rooted in justice, fairness, and equity in the classroom. As the students in Room 405 questioned whether or not to protest, go on strike, or engage in other direct action, I needed to step back so they could determine what was best for themselves.

Further, there are certainly risks for students when they direct curriculum in an effort to solve authentic problems. They lose the protection of contrived lesson plans. Indeed, interaction with the real world can be problematic. Not only is doubt expressed by those who do not think young students (especially students of color and economically disadvantaged students) are capable of effecting change, there are threats of exploitation by outsiders when the curriculum goes beyond the school building.

NEEDING SUPPORT

Key to teaching in accordance with democratic principles and enabling students to be involved in curriculum creation is the support of the administration, colleagues, parents, and the community. What are the administrators willing to permit? What would colleagues support? How could parents and the community become partners with me? Convincing these various people—many exceedingly skeptical—that this type of curriculum was worthwhile and in the students' best interests was paramount to its success. By examining my strategies, as well as the way in which I grounded my risky teaching practice in relevant curriculum studies literature, the means for sustaining my justice-oriented classroom can be better understood.

Administrators

Teachers interested in sustaining social justice teaching must be willing to work with the local school administration. Simultaneously, they need to let administrators know that the teaching and learning taking place may not follow the typical, normative approaches that occur in their schools or in the American educational system. Developing a trusting, reciprocal relationship with the principal and assistant principal was essential to making my vision a reality. Open communication about my ideas and rationale fostered a common trust between the administration and myself. Careful to never come across as preaching or implying that I was on a higher moral ground than other teachers, I demonstrated my actions to the administration rather than telling them about it.

From the beginning, I was quick to invite administrators into the classroom to see what a curriculum based on what students valued most was like. Administrators witnessed firsthand the power of democratic teaching when students interviewed various classroom guests or engaged in a debate. After observing the class's interview of a state senator, the assistant principal wrote, "I was convinced to support you because of your basic approach to the project. . . . The students' enthusiasm was also a convincing aspect."

Further, instead of resisting the commonalities of lesson plans or scheduling routines of the average school day, I complied with these requirements. In these circumstances, I followed the rules, often going beyond the expectations in explanation and illustration. My principal expressed appreciation for the vivid, detailed descriptions.

Truth be told, though, most of these detailed portrayals were developed following the class's engagement. This was not an act of resistance, but rather a result of not knowing what students would focus on in a particular classroom session. I often took detailed notes, kept a reflective journal, and then wrote up the lesson plan or classroom activity after the fact. Since topics were all interwoven, this did not present a problem. I was also prepared when the administration decided to drop in on any given day. This is because I never came to the classroom unprepared. Quite the contrary, I usually had in mind a multitude of ideas, plans, or ways to teach a certain concept or idea. I was willing to adapt based on the momentum of the classroom.

In addition to the detailed lesson plans, I learned to show how the curriculum that we developed met the Illinois Learning Standards. Although I continued to believe that standards were outcomes, rather than front-loaded objectives, connecting what we did to these state mandates was not difficult. Since the nature of the curriculum was so comprehensive, the standards were easily backward-mapped to what we were accomplishing. Making these connections also pleased the administration. The assistant principal described her approval in writing:

> I thought you were crazy at first because your lessons were not as structured as a typical fifth-grade class at Carr. I didn't know how the students would adapt to this, but as the unit grew, and it became

obvious you had a plan, my fears lessened. The structure of the project became apparent, with each ensuing lesson. . . . I became convinced to back you from a pedagogical point of view.

I was also able to garner the administration's backing through the initiatives and grants brought into Carr to broaden Room 405's opportunities. Whether I was developing a mentor partnership via the Web-based Collaboratory with a university across the country, or working with a colleague at a nearby high school to develop an interest-based learning exchange between high school and elementary students, the administrators applauded the creative ways to reach the students. To support these and other endeavors, outside funding was necessary. I applied for grants from various foundations and corporations and secured support from several, including the Chicago Foundation for Education, the Oppenheimer Family Fund, Nike/Jordan Fundamentals, AlphaSmart, Inc., and the National Education Association Foundation for Improvement of Education. But before applying for any grant, taking any initiative, or connecting to any community organization, I always sought permission, input, and guidance from the administration, even though it was not required or expected. Since the administration was supportive of teachers and their visions, I never had to convince them, but, interestingly enough, I observed other teachers who did not take this step and did not have the same support. By making the administration a collaborator with Room 405, I earned its interest in the successes we all shared.

Writing small, anecdotal stories about our classroom endeavors also helped communication with the school administration. My principal mentioned that he enjoyed sharing what was happening at Carr with colleagues at their weekly meetings and that the vignettes were a great way to do it. Differing from lesson plans that focused on scope and sequence, these short narratives allowed the administrators to readily understand our initiatives and easily convey them to others.

Looking to administrators for guidance based on their many years in schools, I made it clear that I wanted to learn from their wisdom. Their breadth of experience and willingness to share undoubtedly helped my teaching. Further, in an interesting role reversal for urban, African American fifth graders, Room 405's fight for a new school building in many ways provided voice to the administration, since, in fact, it had been waiting for the city and board of education to fulfill their promises. One commented,

Room 405 students use AlphaSmart word processors to assist in their letter-writing campaign.

"My confidence as an administrator grew as I began to see the expansion of the project and ideas the students were generating to keep it fresh."

Colleagues

Similarly, I was able to find common ground with colleagues through communication and by proving my commitment to the school and its students. These relationships were not as easy to achieve as those I formed with the administration, since some colleagues were skeptical about new teachers. Most of the teachers at Carr had been there for years, if not decades. Since I came from the corporate world, I am certain many were unsure how I would fare. Most simply waited to pass judgment, especially when several viewed our classroom as being out of control. I recognized that building successful relations with other teachers was taking more time than creating relationships with the administration and that I needed to find alternative ways to build trust.

Spending some of my prep periods in other teachers' classrooms allowed them to view me as an additional resource rather than just another teacher. At the same time, I extended open invitations to colleagues to see what was happening in Room 405. Communication blossomed, and many began to ask questions about my teaching approach. This strategy broke down barriers, and other teachers became more supportive of what one teacher called "the most unusual and bizarre classroom management style." Another teacher, a 20-year veteran at Carr, approached me saying, "I never learned your kind of teaching when I was in school. I am interested in what you are doing since those kids seem so enthusiastic."

Although many colleagues supported me, others challenged my approach. Some teachers thought I was doing a disservice to students because I was not following the textbook. After being told by a colleague that my lessons did not appear to be meeting the all-important standards, I asked her to assist me in aligning them. Her willingness to teach me, along with my willingness to learn, allowed our relationship to grow and develop. She had worked in the school for a long time and had much insight to offer. Before I knew it, she was experimenting with some interest-based classroom activities with her students, and I was applying some of her suggestions.

Parents

Getting the parents' support of my progressive teaching style had its challenges as well. I knew that communication with parents was essential, but I did not have the foresight to see how time-consuming it would be. I kept in contact through newsletters, daily phone calls, and inviting them to the classroom to teach us about their areas of expertise or accompany us on field trips.

When I arrived at Carr, I felt like the ultimate outsider. During my first week teaching, I was walking past the other fifth-grade classroom and overheard a parent scolding her child in the hallway for misbehaving. Out of view, I listened as she told her child that if he did not start behaving, she was going to punish him by sending him "to that new White teacher's room!" Thank goodness those sentiments changed, but it did not happen overnight. Getting parents involved through ongoing communication was key to the success of Room 405. A parent e-mailed me after the school year ended and gave some insight as to why parents were supportive. She wrote, "You always communicated with parents. I was very pleased that you called regularly. . . . Other teachers only called if there was a problem, never if my child was making progress. Thank you!"

I also communicated with parents by writing narrative report cards. Although the Chicago Public Schools required teachers to use a standard grading scale and send home report cards complete with a behavior checklist, I also included multipage narratives about each child. These accounts, co-written with each student, focused on classroom work plus areas of strength and opportunities for improvement. Students had a great deal of input in these letters. Such negotiation allowed the teacher–student relationship to develop. According to Diminor's journal, the narratives were "alright 'cause there be no surprises when my report card gets in my mamma's hands." Not only did we deliberate about what should be included, but the student and I both had to be willing to sign them. Parents would then read, sign, and return the narrative of their child's progress. These became a starting point for dialogue among the students, the parents, and me. They helped build the parental relationship and allowed parents to understand my teaching approach. The reports also created avenues that allowed me to visit the students' homes. Through this communication channel, the parents came to appreciate my immersion in the lives of their children beyond school. Whether at a community barbecue or at the local tutoring center, I made it a point to extend my role beyond that of "typical teacher."

Parents responded well to the written communication. Many stayed in touch consistently throughout the year and beyond. I received a note from one parent over a year after Room 405's triumphant journey explaining why she thought what occurred in Room 405 was successful.

> It was obvious you had confidence in those kids . . . I trusted you to teach the way you did because I knew you had respect for them. The kids came to believe that they were capable of doing anything. Not only did the parents trust you but the kids did too . . . after having you as the leader they all became a family and knew what it felt like to be a part of something.

Curriculum Studies Literature

There is no question that the interest and encouragement of people in the school and community supported and sustained the justice-oriented classroom. In addition to the support from the Carr community, I believe my engagement in doctoral studies throughout the school year helped as well. Doctoral classroom discussions certainly acted as an extended support system.

Historical precedent, as well as the contemporary curriculum studies literature, certainly steered my teaching practice. The importance and richness of those texts helped nurture my experimentation in the classroom. Other teachers may also find similar guidance by examining writing about teaching to assist them in classroom endeavors. Unfortunately, much of my own teacher preparation program, like too many others, reduced teaching to a simplistic "how-to." I received the "Scott-Foresman way of teaching fractions" and the "McGraw-Hill method for phonics," but I was not encouraged to examine the essential writing that discussed the nature of curriculum and learning over the past hundred years.

The teacher education methods courses I took promoted recipes or direct instruction strategies that focused on the latest trends branded by big publishing houses. I was not afforded the opportunity to understand why and how the trends had evolved. By looking back through the literature on American education during my doctoral studies, as detailed in the following sections, I found much resolve. Not only was this an invaluable resource, but it also guided me through my practice, helping me make curricular decisions while I worked with students and colleagues. Even though there were excellent teachers at Carr school, none were practicing progressive teaching the way I envisioned it. The literature helped provide courage, ideas, and sustenance to teach the way I did.

The curriculum studies literature also explained ideas relevant to the current state of affairs and offered hope in light of the frustration teachers feel as a result of demands faced daily. I sincerely recommend that both pre-service and current teachers look to the extensive literature to support their classroom practices. They may learn from these writings, gaining insight into approaches and potentially improving the learning experiences of young people.

THEORIZING WITH STUDENTS

As a teacher, I felt like a theorizer throughout the course of the year and suggest that all teachers are actually theorizers. Each day, and possibly every moment, teachers make decisions, adjust lessons, and attempt to understand the classroom dynamic according to the situation, interests, and needs of their particular students, themselves, and their overall goals for the class. Often, especially in this age of high-stakes testing, teacher-proofing demands that educators deliver canned lessons and read from scripts to meet the supposed needs of their students. Teachers' ability to make decisions based on their best judgment and experiences has been stripped away by the current accountability craze. I did not function well in such prescriptive circumstances and suspect this is the case for many other teachers.

ɔLikewise, students can and do theorize. By allowing space for students to determine what is worthwhile to them, we help them to better meet their own needs and desires while simultaneously achieving on external measurements.

Teachers interested in learning more about the notion of theorizing have both historical and contemporary literature to examine. From a historical perspective, teachers will find the works of John Dewey [including, but certainly not limited to, *Democracy and Education* (1916) and *Experience and Education* (1938)] to be especially helpful in thinking about teachers as theorizers and how teachers, alongside their students, can and do theorize.

In addition, the work of L. Thomas Hopkins suggests how students make self-selections about what and how they learn. It stresses the need for students to be designers of their own curriculum. When Hopkins (1954) questioned what makes the curriculum, he acknowledged that adults outside the classroom are responsible for creating it, but he asserted, in a sentiment that influenced my theories, that "according to their own evidence, however, the learning results are unsatisfactory" (p. 111). Since children make their own self-selections from available materials in the classroom environment, Hopkins (1976) contrasted two kinds of curriculum: the IS, or learning curriculum, with the WAS, or taught curriculum. The WAS curriculum focuses on textbook learning and the acquisition of facts from people who are no longer alive, whereas the IS curriculum is a holistic approach that studies the firsthand experiences of students in the classroom. This conceptualization of how curriculum could be enacted made me realize that the children should be the ones to develop a classroom's curriculum.

Students who are provided this opportunity help redefine the role of students and teachers. No longer is the teacher the supplier of knowledge, filling vessels with already constructed knowledge (Freire, 1970; Freire & Macedo, 2001). Instead, my students became constructors of meaning, vis-à-vis questions they sought to answer, while my role as teacher provided assistance and support in their problem-posing and meaning-making. As a teacher, I needed to change typical knowledge limits, alter subject matters when necessary or appropriate, and, most important, listen to the students, while allowing them freedom to choose those learnings that they deemed most valuable.

Using these ideas to frame my teaching approach, the philosophy of Room 405's social action–oriented project was furthered by my examination of Joseph Schwab's (1978) notion of practical inquiry and the "arts of eclectic" (p. 322). Schwab described practical inquiry as a means of deliberation to develop an engaging curriculum in the context of an actual classroom based on the interplay and interaction of the commonplaces of the school setting: teachers, students, subject matter, and milieu. I was particularly influenced by this concept as well as eclectic arts, or the ability of a teacher to match and subsequently adapt theoretical knowledge with a plurality of perspectives to the wants and interests of students. By adapting and tailoring curricula to the desires of the students, together in Room 405 we developed the capacity to generate alternative courses of action. As a result, we were able to foster learning in our specific classroom, while at the same time we were able to seek higher moral ground in the daily activities in which we found ourselves. This examination of the curricular commonplaces led me to more contemporary writing that discussed the hopeful possibilities of theorizing with my students.

Building on the ideas of Schwab, William H. Schubert's historical and contemporary examination of these ideas opened up an additional area to explore. Schubert's (1989) essay on the practical value of practical inquiry showed that Schwab's ideas could have a place in my contemporary classroom. His work with on conceptualizing teacher lore (1991)—the reflective inquiry-based stories that teachers can share about their own experiences in the act of teaching—as a form of curriculum inquiry further provided a basis to understand that it is indeed promising for teachers to engage in personal theorizing (1992) and for students to be action researchers (1995). Reading these works and wrestling with their ideas highlighted much of what guided and inspired me in the classroom.

EDUCATION WITH AUTHENTICITY AND PURPOSE

Rather than teaching students based on contrived lessons, as I have explained, I strove to construct curriculum with my students, extending decision making to immediate participants rather than outsiders. An integrated curriculum naturally weaves together different subjects, allowing the classroom to lose its compartmentalization by content area. The curriculum is no longer separated into different disciplines; authentic problem solving fluidly incorporates the entire curriculum. If a teacher listens to and follows students' needs, the curriculum cannot only be created by the students but also can subsequently be of and, therefore, for them (Schubert & Lopez Schubert, 1981).

Recent educational reform initiatives have brought many new and different ideas to teaching practices. Many reformers argue that teaching skills in artificially compartmentalized groups or subject disciplines does not prepare students for everyday life, and that an integrative approach to education is necessary to improve the skills of children in the disciplines of knowledge as well as in critical thinking, social, and problem-solving skills that can be leveraged and transferred for ensuing experiences.

The concept of creating integrated curricula is well intended, but there has been much debate about the definition and meaning of integration in the context of a school or classroom. There have been many contemporary examinations that cite an integrated approach to curriculum (e.g., Drake, 1998; Jacobs, 1989). In these cases, however, the definition often pertains to curriculum that merely crosses subject matters to bring different disciplines together. Although this provides the basis for linking parts of the curriculum to reflect an interdependent real world, the substance of this approach does not focus on the making of personal meaning through participation in public life or on student interest, as educational thinkers like Dewey (1938), Hopkins (1937), and Alberty (1947) advocated. Unfortunately, these more recent interpretations put the teacher or the subject matter, rather than the students, at the center of the curriculum. But the students *need* to be the centerpiece. Their interests and their concerns can produce curricula from the initial question "What is something you and the students want to solve?"

Teachers interested in developing spaces for integrative, emergent, and authentic curriculum can look, as I did, to the earlier theorizers for guidance. Dewey stated in *Democracy and Education* (1916) that education needed to come from the interests of the students, rather than from the disciplines themselves. Kilpatrick (1918) built on Dewey's interpretation by developing what he termed a "project-method" in which education and learning proceeded from student interests as opposed to disciplines of knowledge.

The Progressive Education Association's (PEA) Eight-Year Study (1930–1942), one of the most comprehensive educational studies in the last century, also sheds light on these ideas. The experiment highlighted 30 different school systems that used a progressive or integrated approach to teaching and learning—again, based on what was important to the students. Although all but forgotten, many progressive educators consider the Eight-Year Study to be one of the most significant undertakings in educational research. The results indicated that the experimental schools organized around themes related to student interest convincingly outperformed the traditional schools using the disciplines of knowledge and subject-matter approach in achievement and success in life (Aikin, 1942; Kridel & Bullough, 2007).

Similarly, L. Thomas Hopkins argued in 1937 that integration is something that we do innately and posited that this integration is not done by others for us. He contended that integration of curriculum starts with the people involved, since they create or imagine the problem they desire to solve. Contemporary curriculum integration expert James Beane (1991) asserts:

> Integration implies wholeness and unity rather than separation and fragmentation . . . real curriculum integration occurs when young people confront personally meaningful questions and engage in experiences related to those questions—experiences they can integrate into their own system of meanings. (p. 9)

Drawing on the progressive nature of subject matter from this historical, interest-based perspective, Beane (1995) writes, "Curriculum integration begins with the idea that the sources of curriculum ought to be problems, issues, and concerns posed by life itself . . . [the] central focus of curriculum integration is the search for self- and social meaning" (p. 616). It is this form of curriculum integration that pushes the idea of students as the starting point rather than simply linking subject areas together in an aggregated manner. Students integrating curriculum derived from their own questions can utilize critical thinking skills and problem-solving techniques driven by an authentic quest to make meaning in their broader social context (Beane, 1997, 2005).

Curriculum allowing students to integrate and solve relevant questions meaningful to themselves creates a knowledge-rich environment. Students adapt and tailor the knowledge to fit their needs while sharing experiences with peers. They seek to construct and answer their own questions. As students investigate and solve pertinent questions, the innately authentic construction that occurs is contrary to prescriptive curricula that would help control them. With the opportunity to be creators of their own curriculum, students can avoid the typical memorization and rote learning that lack concrete avenues for them to transfer skills broadly to other areas of their lives. The role of the teacher, therefore, can be to assist the students in transferring skills acquired in the classroom into the real world. Connecting the curriculum diminishes the shortcomings of strict subject-matter teaching and educates for understanding.

DEVELOPING CLASSROOMS FOR SOCIAL ACTION

By developing schools and classrooms that are democratic, we encourage students to take the initiative to drive their curriculum needs through integrated and authentic means. A democratic curriculum, allowing children to have a key role in choosing what is most important to them, is essential in providing students and teachers opportunities for achievement while motivating all the participants. Together, the classroom community can strive to engage in democratic action to achieve their mutually decided goals. Further, if there are few barriers to true democratic participation, students often choose to make their curriculum one of social action. They intuitively seek out ways to help the greater good and reach for higher moral ground instead of focusing on simpler tasks, as skeptics claim. Students in Room 405 named ideas like mandatory daily recess as a problem to solve, but instead they chose to focus their energies on larger social issues important to them.

In a democratic classroom, the teacher is afforded the opportunity to learn from, with, and alongside students, rather than being the keeper of knowledge. Students are not treated as docile recipients of information deemed by outsiders as worth knowing. With high-stakes accountability at the forefront in schools today, many teachers and administrators believe democratic classrooms to be impossible. Contrary to these expectations, Room 405 students also achieved on traditional standardized assessments.

The premise that active democracies require sustained dialogue, deliberation, and debate was a critical component to the educational and pedagogic philosophy of Room 405. John Dewey recognized the essential role that public schools can play in teaching these habits of democratic process, stressing that the democratic ideal must encompass every part of public schooling. This is accomplished, in Dewey's view, by public schools that teach thinking processes rather than focus on memorization, regurgitation, and the acquisition of disconnected facts. Schools should work to be representative of miniature communities, thus promoting a democratic ideal throughout society.

Inspired to deliver on Dewey's writing about the democratic ideal and the role of the public school, I looked to more contemporary scholars' writing about democracy in today's schools. The work of William Ayers (2004) echoes the call for such an ideal and pushed me to examine my ethical and moral capacity as a teacher to make our classroom a community in the literal sense. Further, I was particularly influenced by Michael Apple and James Beane's (2007) argument that "Democratic schools, like democracy itself, do not happen by chance. They result from explicit attempts by educators to put in place arrangements and opportunities that will bring democracy to life" (p. 9). It was essential to allow the children to become part of the curriculum making, by following democratic principles and encouraging engagement in a democratic experience. Otherwise, the classroom and its structures can dehumanize students.

To promote the democratic classroom, I understood that student involvement was paramount. Administrators—or even I, as the teacher—could not make all decisions. With constant and looming probationary threats due to accountability factors, the teachers in schools serving the poorest neighborhoods are under the most pressure to conform. The focus on improving test scores for these schools often means that "minority children are more likely than their peers to spend time taking multiple choice standardized tests and to be taught a low-level curriculum designed around these tests—all in the name of 'raising standards,' of course" (Feinberg, 1997, p. 32).

Our yearlong classroom initiative offered the students of Room 405 the chance not only to participate in mainstream political and democratic activities but also to challenge that mainstream by actively engaging in a public campaign as they sought to get a new school building for their community. The class project provided the opportunity for the students to enact Dewey's (1916) definition of democracy as "a mode of associated living, of conjoint communicated experience" (p. 93), realizing what democracy is really all about.

One of the primary purposes of American public schools is to prepare children to be good and productive citizens. Unfortunately, most students do not have any opportunity to develop or practice these skills as part of a typical school experience. Schools often promote democratic citizenship education by requiring students to memorize specific facts and study attributes of local, state, and federal government. Learning about the three levels of government is quite different from enacting and participating in democratic life itself. In order for students to have the skills necessary to engage in democratic and civic participation and transfer the skills beyond the classroom, they need to have direct involvement as part of their regular school curriculum.

If one accepts that practicing democratic decision making is necessary for students to become active civic participants, the essential question is raised about what it means to teach good citizenship. While trying to answer this question in relation to the endeavors of Room 405, I sought out varying viewpoints related to what "educating the 'good' citizen" encompassed and the broad "spectrum of what good citizenship is and what good citizens do" (Westheimer & Kahne, 2004, p. 237). It is no wonder that teachers often avoid the engaging, democratic ways of teaching citizenship—there are inherent risks involved in providing the space for students to practice citizenship, allowing the students to focus on what is most important to them.

Teachers who encourage and foster school opportunities for students to be what Freire (1970) termed critical readers of their world encourage citizenship in the classroom setting. This initiation into active citizenship provides students with the necessary means to transfer skills to other experiences beyond the classroom. By promoting direct participation in civic life and politics, teachers go beyond the notion of a good citizen as simply being responsible and good to others; instead, they encourage children to be active players in curricula and society. Furthermore, these educators challenge the neutrality of the typical citizenship curricula commonplace in public schools, in an effort to promote change as a fundamental aspect of classroom learning and democratic living.

PROGRESSIVE EDUCATION IN DISADVANTAGED NEIGHBORHOODS

Progressive educational practices are possible in schools serving poor neighborhoods. Typically, students in the lower socioeconomic classes, especially in inner-city schools populated mostly by African American and Latino children, are expected to follow the rules and give the right answers.

Teachers in these schools are expected to instruct their students in a regimented manner, thus conforming to a hidden curriculum based on social class (Anyon, 1980). By leveraging past examples of successful progressive educational ideals triumphing in disadvantaged areas, the students and I showed that nontraditional techniques, which avoid skill-and-drill practices, can meet (and often exceed) outside expectations. By challenging the notion that students from disadvantaged areas are not capable or are not interested in their education, the examples detailed below can lay a foundation for future endeavors.

In American classrooms, it is unfortunately customary that only affluent students have the opportunity to think for themselves and receive creative teaching. This idea suggests that only middle- and upper-class children are able to respond to the curriculum questions of what is most worthwhile. Based on their affluence, there is a belief that these students will have choices in their own lives and should begin making them in school. But, the reasoning goes, students of lower-socioeconomic families will not have these choices as they grow up, so there is no reason for them to practice decision making in school.

Why does this occur? Can progressive concepts be successful if introduced into schools that serve marginalized neighborhoods? Can schools serving poor neighborhoods provide the same opportunities as ones that have vast resources and a different view of student capabilities? I found my answers to these essential questions by focusing on the Deweyan ideal of democratic education and its role in community building.

From 1896 to 1903, John Dewey's Laboratory School at the University of Chicago challenged public education practices. Dewey wanted to create a school that was a cooperative community in which students could satisfy their inquisitive minds. He believed that any student was capable of responding to this approach to learning and could participate in this type of dialectic instruction regardless of socioeconomic status.

Contending that in order to embody the democratic ideal, schools need to embrace all learners equally, Dewey posited that the manner in which schools were currently structured continued to promote a superior class. All students, no matter their background, are capable of participating in a progressive curriculum. Successful implementation of progressive approaches can be achieved in poor communities by adhering to the progressive ideas about this alternative approach to education. Although the demands for accountability have escalated since Dewey's time, I felt there was hope for my goal of fostering the progressive educational ideals in a school serving the Cabrini Green neighborhood.

Successful progressive educational projects have been achieved. The Eight-Year Study (described earlier in this chapter) showed that experimental schools in any kind of environment outperformed traditional schools on virtually all criteria (Aiken, 1942; Kridel & Bullough, 2007). The Small Schools Workshop (2007), an organization and movement that began in 1995, is a wonderful example of success in creating new, small, innovative learning communities in public schools on the premise that "small schools can create a more intimate learning environment that is better able to address the needs of those within the school" (online). Another example is Deborah Meier's (1996) work at the Central Park East school in East Harlem and the Mission Hill School in Boston, demonstrating democracy in action in inner-city public schools. George Wood's (2005) Federal Hocking High School in rural Ohio is exemplary of progressive educational ideals working in poor communities. The Foxfire approach to teaching and learning and Foxfire's numerous books and magazines provide another hopeful example of progressive curriculum strategies that are "characterized by student involvement and action, by thoughtful reflection and rigorous assessment, by imaginations and problem solving, and by meaningful connections to the community" in poor, underserved, and disadvantaged neighborhoods (Foxfire, 2007, online).

Students in disadvantaged neighborhoods can counter the authoritative practices common in many poor schools by creating situations that "trust people's ability to develop their capacity for working collectively to solve their own problems" (Horton, Kohl, & Kohl, 1997). This approach, promoted by Myles Horton at the Highlander Folk School in Tennessee during the height of the civil rights movement, exemplifies a nurturing environment that allows its students to engage in the informed action of praxis—putting theoretical knowledge based on specific values into practice—that embraces the students' activism and reflection based on their priority concerns.

The important question to be asked here is: If this has been shown to be successful, why is progressive education not put into practice elsewhere? The back-to-basics movement and the importance of obedience to authority as necessities for teaching the poor are certainly contributing factors. Policy makers, politicians, and proponents of traditional, content-based teaching see schooling in poor, urban schools as the transmission of cultural knowledge "from the teacher (who has it) to the child (who doesn't), a process that relies on getting the child to listen to lectures, read textbooks, and often, to practice skills by completing worksheets" (Kohn, 1999, online).

Blacks and Latinos, who comprise the majority of students in poor schools in the inner city, are exposed to drill-and-kill and teaching-to-the-test curricula because policy makers believe that urban children are not able to engage in the problem posing, interest-based questioning, and critical thinking inherent in progressive curricula (Berliner & Biddle, 1995). Unfortunately, this belief reinforces the conviction that certain children need to be taught in certain ways dependent on their class.

Mainstream and popularized educational theorists such as E. D. Hirsch Jr. (1987) and Diane Ravitch (2000) oppose progressive education practices. Although they claim ideological neutrality, their views on progressive education are regularly utilized by conservative policy makers. They posit that progressive education does not provide the strategies necessary for all learners, especially disadvantaged ones.

Hirsch (1987) argues that a scripted curriculum will lessen the gap between races by establishing "guideposts that can be of practical use to teachers, students, and all others who need to know our literate culture" (p. 140). What Hirsch fails to acknowledge is that students in poor schools are a product of transferring existing social norms from generation to generation through what Michael Apple calls cultural reproduction (1995), and simply memorizing decontextualized facts will not prepare, motivate, or keep students interested in school.

Similarly, Ravitch's (2000) historical critique of the progressive education movement "recounts the story of unrelenting attacks on the academic mission of schools" (pp. 14–15). Asserting that the progressive education movement has deprived students, especially poor ones, of academic rigor is not only misleading, it is incorrect. Teachers ought to be aware of these inaccurate, misguided critiques. With Ravitch's and Hirsch's current popularity, especially through the prepackaged, fact-based Core Knowledge Foundation curriculum series that has been adopted by a multitude of urban school districts, teachers desiring to teach in democratic ways are certain to face an uphill battle.

COMPLICATING GOOD INTENTIONS

Race, class, and privilege were important factors in my teaching practice and my drive to bring a developmental democracy and problem-posing curriculum to students in a school serving a poor community. My own worries about imposing my experiences and values on the students, as well as my examination of my own assumptions and biases, provided context for me to engage in theorizing with them. With a commitment to building relationships in my classroom and with the community, I pursued ways to learn about their daily lives as an admitted outsider. I saw myself in many ways as a student of my students—able to learn from them by sharing authority in the classroom and allowing them to teach me. I struggled with writing about the students, school, and community, since I understood that what and how I represented everything came from my singular perspective. How did my outsider status affect my ability to express myself about such matters?

As part of the dominant cultural group in the United States, how was I, as a teacher, able to reconcile my identity, connect with students, and ultimately teach for social justice? Seeking to contextualize the experiences of the students, I consider what was emphasized and omitted in my own education and how my lived experiences growing up contribute to my present worldview. I examined how my current understanding of multicultural education informs my behavior and how my perceptions about the racial and cultural "other" reflect my personal background to help me better understand the complexity of my experiences (see Grant & Sleeter, 2007).

The complicated nature of race was, and continues to be, important to the examination of my teaching practice. In order to promote, advocate, and facilitate a just classroom, I examined writing about culturally relevant pedagogy and culturally responsive teaching. I problematize race not to arrive at a conclusion or judge whether the differences are good or bad, right or wrong, but instead to better understand my role as a teacher and what it takes for me to connect with my students.

Historically, progressive approaches have rarely addressed the inherent power dynamics that exist when White teachers work with students of color. These students' communities and schools lack the access and resources that a White, middle-class, male teacher like myself had previously accepted as commonplace. Reading works by Carter G. Woodson (1933), W. E. B. DuBois (1903), and Booker T. Washington (1901) pushed me to better understand from a historical perspective how racial identity is constructed and why it was important in my classroom. This investigation led to more recent examinations of how power dynamics play an essential role in today's schooling and overall educational system.

My descriptions, throughout this book, of Carr Academy as disadvantaged come from my cultural perspective. This perspective was inherently privileged, especially in regard to my educational upbringing and experiences. It raises valid questions that must be addressed: From whose viewpoint are the neighborhoods "disadvantaged"? Why are they disadvantaged? Is it appropriate for me to want to advocate for my ideas, or better yet, my ideals of what these particular African American students in my classroom should have in their education?

My reading of Lisa Delpit challenged my progressive teaching orientation. Her critique of White educators from the dominant culture who think they know best how to educate students of color resonated strongly with me. Delpit's (2006) prose frequently made me question my teaching approach. Her almost accusatory style made me look at a bigger picture, so the minority students in my classroom could "be taught the codes needed to participate fully in the mainstream of American life" (p. 45). This was essential to the underlying processes my students and I engaged in throughout our learning. Delpit's argument challenged me to rethink my progressive education strategies and seemingly good intentions to assure that my students got the skills necessary to matriculate.

I believed the progressive models would work with my students as a means for growth, allowing them to transcend going "to school to find out what other people have done, and then go out in life to imitate them" (Woodson, 1933, p. 138), but I also believed I could not do this alone, heeding Delpit's (2006) assertion "that appropriate education for poor children and children of color can only be devised in consultation with adults who share their culture" (p. 45).

At first offended by what seemed to be attacks on me as a White teacher in Delpit's work, I came to believe that too often teachers focus on making teaching conform to perceived "best practices" and miss the opportunity to actually get to know and reach their students. In my desire to teach against the tradition that Woodson (1933) described, in which "Negroes have not control over their education and have little voice in their affairs pertaining thereto" (p. 22), I reflected on what I had read, understanding that some of these progressive tactics alone were not providing the students access to what they really needed. It was imperative for me to teach codes of power, provide access to Standard English and other skills that would help the children in the classroom to achieve in their future, and approach teaching in what Gloria Ladson-Billings (1994) describes as a culturally relevant way.

I had to actively listen and consciously learn from and with my students so that together we could find the means necessary to explore the processes in which we engaged. Beyond this reading, listening, and learning, I came to understand that I knew very little about the students' daily lives. I sought out ways to delve deeper into their lived experiences by visiting students' homes, meetings with parents in and out of school, and becoming active in the community.

One of the first realities I needed to address was the cultural difference that existed between my students and myself. Overcoming the discomfort and awkwardness of discussing the differences with my students was not easy. In the beginning, I often felt uncomfortable deliberating about this because I felt that by admitting I reflected the dominant culture in their classroom, I was creating a divide. Initially, I attempted to be colorblind, but I soon felt even more awkward, sensing that I was attempting to "erase our racial categories, ignore differences, and thereby achieve an illusionary state of sameness or equality" (Howard, 2006, p. 57). I needed to discuss our differences in the classroom. By listening to their experiences and presenting mine, I could hear them, we could share experiences, and I could learn from them ways in which I could help make learning relevant. My exposure to the texts helped me understand cultural relevance and make sense of what Joyce King (1991) refers to as "dysconcious racism" (p. 133).

With dialogue about race occurring, there were open discussions about our differences. This openness allowed for the students to assert their needs and interests in problems they felt needed to be solved. Consequently, they attacked the issue of inequity and issues of power when provided with the opportunity, even amidst the notion "that a Black student with a book is acting White" (Obama, 2004). Whereas I do not believe I was encouraging Whiteness, I saw how this could have been perceived by my students or others in the school or community.

In my effort to confront and acknowledge White dominance, I turned to Gary Howard's writing as I worked to teach against the notion of White savior. As a White multicultural educator, Howard's account of his personal and professional journey toward understanding racial identity in _We Can't Teach What We Don't Know_ (2006) had a profound effect on me as it forced me to examine the often-overlooked nature of White dominance. Learning to challenge the excuse of colorblindness all too common of White teachers educating Black children, I became more aware of how racial and class issues presented themselves in the classroom. Problematizing race, class, and privilege with students, and on my own, allowed me to become a better teacher and work to challenge the inequities inherent to our current state of affairs.

Sustaining and supporting justice-oriented teaching is challenging, yet possible. Teachers need to seek out various avenues to gain support for their visions of social justice in schools. By partnering and building relationships with administrators, colleagues, and parents, in addition to getting involved in the broader school community, I was able to sustain my unorthodox teaching. Beyond the human support, literature served as an inspirational guide to my classroom practice. Literature was an indispensable resource, model, justification, and support mechanism. Utilizing various means of support and curriculum literature is essential to beginning and sustaining social justice teaching endeavors.

7

Conclusion

A photo opportunity with Project Citizen director Michael Fischer at the Center for Civic Education Conference.

HOW YA GONNA HELP US?

The students' faces lit up with intensity as the airplane accelerated down the runway. It was the October following our incredible fifth-grade year, and my former students were on the trip of a lifetime. The students from Room 405 were about to show off their unbelievable curriculum to a national audience. They had been invited to present at the Center for Civic Education's (CCE) National Conference. The students were the only school-aged group selected from classrooms nationwide to represent the problem-based, service learning initiative Project Citizen. Due to their unprecedented efforts of leveraging multiple media and breaking down the typical curriculum barriers found in most classrooms, CCE had offered the students, one parent, and myself an all-expenses-paid trip to present their curriculum. Several months earlier, while the students were steadfastly implementing their action plan, the class had received a surprise visit from a national coordinator of Project Citizen. Without prior notice, the guest stopped by Room 405 to see firsthand what he had been hearing about in the media. He explained that he wanted to pay tribute to them and see them in action, as he was over-whelmed with the fifth graders' participatory involvement in seeking their goal. After listening as students explained the various initiatives they were working on, he praised them as his "heroes" and eagerly questioned them about their democratic action. Because their co-created curriculum had broken down the barriers of the top-down, centralized, and mandated curriculum, he had decided they should be the keynote speakers at the CCE national conference to be held in St. Louis in the fall. This opportunity was vindication for the work our class had done.

This trip would prove to be one of the most rewarding experiences for me as a teacher. Not only were my students selected for their valiant efforts at public policy change, they were also recognized for their com-mitment to helping themselves and their community. Apparently, there had never before been a class whose Project Citizen efforts had encom-passed an entire year's curriculum. And never before had the Center for Civic Education seen a curriculum that had been so driven by students. This recognition, in and of itself, would have been a rewarding experience, but the actual presentation the former Room 405 students delivered to an audience of over 600 adults exceeded my wildest expectation; it provided a capstone to our yearlong endeavors of theorizing together.

As the national director of the center's educational programming in-troduced the Carr students, he remarked:

> We have never before seen any group of young citizens create such a vigorous attempt . . . at integrating curriculum at such a sophisticated level. The work they do shows that there can be rich curriculum even in this era of standardization.

The students gave updated speeches similar to the ones they presented at their Project Citizen hearings and during Ralph Nader's visit. Standing before the vast audience in a hotel conference center, the new sixth graders told their story. Weaving technology throughout, the presentation included their video documentaries, slide shows, and a PowerPoint presentation, and it concluded with an interactive tour of their student-developed Web site. Not only were they inspirational in demonstrating what it meant to co-create a curriculum with their teacher, they also showcased the work that they had accomplished along the way.

Sitting in the audience, I felt like a proud parent as the students showed everyone all that they had done. Along with the conference participants, I marveled at what these extraordinary students had achieved. Seeing their work as a spectator had a different effect on me. These children had moved beyond the limits of my classroom and were able to transfer the competencies they had developed throughout the previous school year. The presentation was a testament to their ability to transfer learning and apply what they had learned to new and different settings.

Acting like old pros, they were not affected by the numerous interruptions of applause. At the end of the presentation, the audience gave a rousing standing ovation. Holding their heads high, the students received the credit and accolades they deserved. For me, this experience illustrated what it means to provide the opportunity and space for students to set their own priorities and be co-creators in curriculum development. This occasion allowed their voices to be heard, and it was magnificent to have them so well recognized.

Their presentation was an indication that the curriculum they had had a hand in developing went beyond the classroom. Although their experience in St. Louis can be considered a crowning moment to the entire previous year, one particular occurrence during their presentation deserves highlighting. Admittedly, while the students were being applauded by the conference participants, I was a little worried, watching the students scribble on their little pads of paper. The skeptical teacher in me was afraid that they were not paying attention and wondered what would happen when it was time for the audience to ask questions. Based on my location in the room and the fact that I was no longer their teacher in the formal sense, I was forced to let the situation play itself out.

As the last student demonstrated the Web site to the audience, I feared that the others were going to be unprepared for the questioning that would soon occur. But as the emcee approached the podium to thank the students and invite audience questions, Malik pulled her away from the microphone. Fearful of what Malik was saying in her ear and knowing from past experiences that he was more than capable of being inappropriate, I found the butterflies of anxiety overtaking me. Apparently, whatever Malik had said to her was convincing enough since she explained to the audience that "instead of having questions from the legislators and all of you, Malik would like to address you all again."

As I apprehensively waited for what he was going to say, Malik, dressed in his perfectly pressed pinstriped suit, retook the microphone. This moment was the climax of the entire student-driven curriculum. Standing behind the podium (which he could barely see over), Malik exclaimed, "Before you ask us any questions, I have a few questions for all of you!" As the audience laughed at his candid approach, Malik was continuing to enact his passion for problem posing, seeking out that which was most important and meaningful to him. Glancing down at the pad of paper where he had written down notes, Malik asked the audience what they thought about his class's hard work. The children had not, in fact, been doodling—they had actually developed their own questions for the audience while they were presenting!

As the audience cheered and clapped, Malik politely interrupted to make an important point: "It is fine and good that y'all think we did good work, 'cause I agree, we did. Thank you. But how ya gonna help us?" The audience suddenly grew silent as he continued:

> You know it costs a lot of money to get a new school, and kids can't go to schools like our bootleg, old one. I am not saying we want your money now, but when you leave out of here, I bet there are schools just like Carr in y'all cities. What are you going to do to make a difference for them kids and them schools? You can't just think we did good, clap a lot—which I like, by the way—and then not do something in your communities. Think about it.

Malik's exemplary series of questions were a perfect manifestation of what we as a class had striven to create the entire previous school year—a problem-posing curriculum that centered around questions that were most important to the students and their lives. Well aware that there were going to be many questions from the audience, Malik also understood that he could think critically for himself. Malik's story illustrates the emergent themes that came out of Carr's Room 405 and the many possibilities for the future of the students and their curriculum.

UNDERSTANDING EACH OTHER

When the classroom is shared and the curriculum is co-constructed, the participants see common threads among and are able to support one another because they have knowledge of others' strengths and weaknesses as well as likes and dislikes. The ability to support one another in classroom activities is important, and this becomes a life skill that can be transferred outside of the classroom and the school environment. Part of understanding one another is the notion of imposing culture or forcing values, norms, and ideas from one's own experiences on others. Did I impose my educational experiences and values of what was worthwhile on the students in my classroom? My hope is that I was not merely trying to take the learning experiences of my culture and place them into the world of my students. Rather, I saw the experiences I had as beneficial to my growth and learning and felt that they could also be helpful in allowing my students to grow.

Although I taught against the imposition of personal ideals, the question of why certain groups of people are given opportunities not afforded to others raises serious questions about teaching and learning. In terms of allowing progressive educational ideals to enter a school serving a poor community, the students (in this case) were able not only to obtain the skills that were required of them by outside mandates, they were also able to gain self-confidence by engaging in a real-life problem that sought an authentic end result. The applications of the curriculum had a purpose that the students were able to recognize. They provided the students with tangible experiences through their own curiosity and theorizing that could be transferred to other situations.

There must be a balance between the students getting what they need and what they think is most important. I often wondered how providing the students with the possibilities of a humanizing curriculum that allowed them to ask meaningful questions would affect them in the future. Could a skill-rich curriculum adhere to democratic principles and progressive educational ideals and vice versa? Isn't one purpose of education to provide students with the opportunity to explore with what they already have: curiosity, intelligence, and the drive not only to achieve but also to make a difference in their own lives? Teachers should embrace the moral obligation to provide them with the skills necessary to matriculate, while also allowing them to explore their world and become conscious, active citizens in the process.

Teachers who open their classrooms to social action and justice-oriented teaching always run the risk of imposing their own values, politics, and desires on their students. This can be the case for all curricula, but it becomes more publicly visible when the curriculum extends beyond the walls of the classroom and into the community. The idea of imposition can be negotiated by making sure there is constant dialogue and deliberation in the classroom. Teachers can best understand the needs of their students by asking them questions and allowing the children, in turn, to pose questions back. Room 405 constantly adapted based on the problems that the students investigated. Much of what was accomplished during the school year was not based on any past experiences that either the students or I had had; rather, it was a direct result of the students engaging with the ideas that seemed most relevant and interesting to them. I had never before done the activities that we engaged in together, but I was willing to be a student alongside my students as we learned together. I needed to become humble in order to grow in my role as a teacher, for I had to become open to building relationships with my students and allowing them to bring ideas in from the outside.

Educators need to realize that there is a constant interplay between themselves and their students as well as the materials of the curriculum and all the contextual factors of the environment and the community. By negotiating among each of these, educators and students can find the curriculum and classroom space stimulating and worthy of their time and energy. Instead of the teacher always presenting received knowledge, the teacher and students can discover the knowledge and experience it together.

LET THOSE VOICES BE HEARD!

Our construction of a classroom based on democratic participation and community action yielded what could be termed a counternarrative. The curriculum that was enacted in our classroom allowed my students to use their voices in a purposeful way that allowed them to be heard. Their message beyond the classroom was clear and contradicted what was typically prescribed for students growing up in an urban housing project. The curriculum that centered on the students' needs engaged them in civic and social action and showed that they were truly concerned about where and how they learned. It went against many of the stereotypes common to urban Black children growing up in the inner city. In many ways, the project opened the eyes of the broader community and offered an invitation into the world of the students at Carr Community Academy. The co-created, justice-oriented curriculum showed that these intelligent young citizens care for themselves, their families, and their community.

A curriculum based on students' priority concerns can have a lasting effect on the students involved and can also help to shape our world. Students interested in making their world a better place motivate themselves as well as increase awareness of the inequity in schooling via their actions. In this case politicians and the media became aware of these needs, and ordinary citizens rose to the occasion. These students successfully showed their fortitude and their promise. They were able to prove to the outside world that they are worth everyone's attention. Most important, though, the project allowed them to see for themselves their multitude of abilities, intelligences, imaginations, and worth. My hope is that this counternarrative has a lasting effect on the students and that they, too, realize, understand, and practice the promises of democracy and active civic engagement.

It is impossible to know what will become of the students from Room 405. But if the actions of Malik and his peers in St. Louis are any indication of what is to come, I am hopeful that the memories, the artifacts, and the learning that they took from this experience will continue to remind them of their spectacular capabilities. As change and displacement continue in the Cabrini Green community, I believe that the students of Room 405 will recall the ways in which they spoke up for what they believed in and understand how they are able to read their own worlds and be active and engaged citizens.

Realizing classroom democratic ideals may raise more questions than answers, I wonder where this sort of curriculum could and would go if it were to be commonly practiced. What would its implications be? Will long-term continuation of a problem-posing curriculum eventually lead some students, especially poor students of color, to be slapped down by the system? While I cannot answer these questions directly, I would like to believe that all students should have space to be thinkers, doers, designers, and builders, challenging the ideological dominance of standardization, accountability, and high-stakes measures. I want to believe that if enough teachers look to their students for what is worthwhile, society as a whole can begin to make our world a better place. I strongly believe that teachers, along with their students, can construct meaningful curricula to challenge inequities and provide opportunities. Much can be gained through individual experimentation with democratic and justice-oriented teaching, and great reflection, change, and transformation can result.

ENDURING ACHIEVEMENT AND IMPACT

Students no longer walk the halls at the Carr Community Academy, yet the building remains standing. Carr has an even more eerie presence than it did while we occupied it. With the high-priced condominiums and town-houses built around the school property in every direction, the redevelopment plan is well under way; Cabrini Green is being transformed. Rumors about the fate of the building abound. Reports indicate the Chicago Board of Education has put the property on the auction block, but apparently it is still holding out for a better offer of more millions before letting it go.

After Carr was closed, the majority of the Room 405 class transferred to the nearby Cresswell school in the Cabrini Green neighborhood. As residential buildings were demolished, families were forced out of the neighborhood attendance area, and the displaced students were relocated to different schools.

Although the class members are now located throughout the city, many former students and I meet or talk regularly. We enjoy updating each other on our lives while recalling our fifth-grade year together. The majority of Room 405 students are now completing the eighth grade, although two students—able to skip seventh grade because of high performance—are now finishing their freshman years at Chicago high schools.

Although it is more than 3 years since the fifth-grade year ended, the students continue to chronicle their story. And they continue to get an exuberant reception from those who hear Room 405's triumphant tale. Neither the students nor I have forgotten what our foray into school and city politics did for us. Together, over the past 3 years, we have presented at several conferences, been guest speakers in numerous college classrooms, and keynoted seminars. Recently we presented a session on how elementary students could use documentary research as an agent of change at the Annual Meeting of the American Educational Research Association.

A follow-up article on the students' push for justice appeared in the *Chicago Tribune* after an education reporter watched their conference presentation (Dell' Angela, 2007). The reporter featured five former Carr fifth graders. Each described the impact the fifth-grade curriculum has had on their lives. Crown, the former fourth-grade truant turned B-average high school student, was quoted: "If it wasn't for that project, I wouldn't be in high school. I'd be out on the block, I know I would" (p. B1).

Other students shared similar sentiments about how the project continues to impact them in multiple ways. But beyond rhetoric, their achievement records and commitment to learning speak for themselves. The class was featured in a high school social studies textbook. Terrance won a districtwide Scripps-Howard Spelling Bee championship as an eighth grader. Tyrone, Jaris, Shaniqua, and Diminor consistently made the honor roll at their respective schools. Dyneisha, Malik, and Tavon hope to attend small specialty high schools in the fall.

Several students also continue to be involved in activism and change efforts in their communities. A few former Room 405 students have applied for a summer program reflective of the civil rights 1964 Mississippi Freedom School. These students want to continue to learn skills about community organizing and about what it means to embrace responsibilities; they also want to engage in methods that promote change to make our world a better place. As the students continue practicing strategies of active democratic participation, they demonstrate that their fifth-grade year, when they fought for what they believed was right, can and is being transferred to other situations they encounter in their lives.

References

Aikin, W. M. (1942). *The story of the Eight-Year Study*. New York: Harper & Brothers.

Alberty, H. A. (1947). *Reorganizing the high school curriculum*. New York: Macmillan.

Anyon, J. (1980). Social class and the hidden curriculum of work. *Journal of Education, 162*(1), 67–92.

Apple, M. W. (1995). *Education and power* (2nd ed.). New York: Routledge.

Apple, M. W., & Beane, J. A. (2007). *Democratic schools* (2nd ed.). Portsmouth, NH: Heinemann.

Ayers, W. C. (2004). *Teaching toward freedom: Moral commitment and ethical action in the classroom*. Boston: Beacon Press.

Ayers, W. C., Hunt, J. A., & Quinn, T. (Eds.). (1998). *Teaching for social justice: A democracy and education reader*. New York: Teachers College Press.

Baldwin, J. (1963). A talk to teachers. *Saturday Review, 46*, 42–44.

Beane, J. A. (1991). The middle school: The natural home of integrated curriculum. *Educational Leadership, 49*(2), 9–13.

Beane, J. A. (1995). Curriculum integration and the disciplines of knowledge. *Phi Delta Kappan, 76*(8), 616–622.

Beane, J. A. (1997). *Curriculum integration: Redesigning the core of democratic education*. New York: Teachers College Press.

Beane, J. A. (2005). *A reason to teach: Creating classrooms of dignity and hope*. Portsmouth, NH: Heinemann.

Berliner, D. C., & Biddle, B. J. (1995). *The manufactured crisis: Myths, fraud, and the attack on America's public schools*. Reading, MA: Addison-Welsey.

Bigelow, B., Christensen, L., Karp, S., Miner, B., & Peterson, B. (1994). *Rethinking our classrooms: Teaching for equity and justice*. Milwaukee, WI: Rethinking Schools.

Brady, M. (2004, May 22). Priceless lesson: Teacher, students put learning into action, show what can be done. *Orlando Sentinel*, p. A19.

Chethik, J. (2004, Spring). Project Citizen at Carr Academy: Fifth graders tackle a big problem. *The Legal Circle, Constitutional Rights Foundation Chicago*, p. 8.

Chicago Public Schools. (1999). *Capital improvement*. Retrieved January 10, 2004, from http://www.csc.cps.k12.il.us/capital/1999book/es/es 2560.html

Chicago Public Schools. (2004). *Chicago Public Schools*. Retrieved June 5, 2004, from http://www.cps.edu/AboutCPS/PressReleases/index.html

Csikszentmihalyi, M. (1990). *Flow: The psychology of optimal experience*. New York: Harper & Row.

Dell' Angela, T. (2007, April 26). School gone, lessons live on: Though they lost the fight to save their campus, Cabrini youths say the effort changed their lives. *Chicago Tribune*, p. B1.

Delpit, L. (2006). *Other people's children: Cultural conflict in the classroom* (2nd ed.). New York: New Press.

Dewey, J. (1916). *Democracy and education*. New York: Free Press.

Dewey, J. (1938). *Experience and education*. New York: Macmillan.

Drake, S. (1998). *Creating integrated curriculum*. Thousand Oaks, CA: Corwin Press.

DuBois, W. E. B. (1903). *The souls of Black folk*. Chicago: McClurg.

Feinberg, W. (1997). Educational manifestos and the new fundamentalism. *Educational Researcher, 26*(8), 27–35.

Foxfire (2007). *Foxfire*. Retrieved March 1, 2007 from http://foxfire.org

Freire, P. (1970). *Pedagogy of the oppressed*. New York: Seabury.

Freire, A. M. A., & Macedo, D. (Eds.). (2001). *The Paulo Freire reader*. New York: Continuum.

Gewertz, C. (2004, July 14). Urban education: Reality 101. *Education Week*, p. 10.

Glass, I. (Producer). (2004, April 16). *This American life (Desperate measures*, Episode 213) [Radio broadcast]. Chicago: National Public Radio.

Grant, C. A., & Sleeter, C. E. (2007). *Doing multicultural education for achievement and equity*. New York: Routledge.

Hirsch, E. D., Jr. (1987). *Cultural literacy: What every American needs to know*. New York: Vintage.

Hoffman, J. (1992). Critical reading/thinking across the curriculum: Using I-charts to support learning. *Language Arts, 69*(2), 121–127.

Hopkins, L. T. (Ed.). (1937). *Integration: Its meaning and application*. New York: Appleton-Century.

Hopkins, L. T. (1954). *The emerging self in school and home*. New York: Harper & Brothers.

Hopkins, L. T. (1976). The WAS vs. the IS curriculum. *Educational Leadership, 34*(3), 211–216.

Horton, M., Kohl, J., & Kohl, H. R. (1997). *The long haul: An autobiography*. New York: Teachers College Press.

Howard, G. (2006). *We can't teach what we don't know: White teachers, multiracial schools* (2nd ed.). New York: Teachers College Press.

Isaac, K. (1992). *Civics for democracy: A journey for teachers and students*. Washington, DC: Center for Study of Responsive Law and Essential Information.

Jacobs, H. H. (Ed.). (1989). *Interdisciplinary curriculum: Design and implementation*. Alexandria, VA: Association for Supervision and Curriculum Development.

Joravsky, B. (2004, June 18). School's out forever. *Chicago Reader, 33*(38), 5–7.

Kilpatrick, W. H. (1918). The project method. *Teachers College Record, 19*(4), 319–335.

King, J. E. (1991). Dysconscious racism: Ideology, identity, and the miseducation of teachers. *Journal of Negro Education, 60*(2), 133–146.

Kohn, A. (1999). Forward . . . into the past. *Rethinking Schools, 14*(1). Retrieved January 15, 2004, from http://www.rethinkingschools.org/archive/14_01/past141.shtml

Kozol, J. (1992). *Savage inequalities: Children in America's schools.* New York: HarperPerennial.

Kridel, C., & Bullough, R. V. (2007). *Stories of the Eight-Year Study: Reexaminig secondary education in America.* Albany: State University of New York Press.

Kumashiro, K. (2002). *Troubling education: Queer activism and antioppressive pedagogy.* New York: RoutledgeFalmer.

Ladson-Billings, G. (1994). *The dreamkeepers: Successful teachers of African American children.* San Francisco: Jossey-Bass.

Lewis, B. A., Espeland, P., & Pernu, C. (1998). *The kid's guide to social action: How to solve the social problems you choose—and turn creative thinking into positive action.* Minneapolis, MN: Free Spirit Publishing.

Meier, D. (1996). *The power of their ideas: Lessons for America from a small school in Harlem.* Boston: Beacon.

Nader, R. (2004a, April 20). Fifth-grade students at a crumbling Chicago elementary school challenge political indifference. *CommonDreams.* Retrieved April 20, 2004, from http://www.commondreams.org/views04/0420-09.htm

Nader, R. (2004b). *The good fight.* New York: Regan Books.

Nader, R. (2004c, June 12). Unpublished manuscript.

Obama, B. (2004, July 27). *Keynote address, Democratic National Convention.* Retrieved August 30, 2004, from http://www.pbs.org/newshour/vote2004/demconvention/speeches/obama.html

Ogle, D. M. (1986). K-W-L: A teaching model that develops active reading of expository text. *Reading Teacher, 39,* 564–570.

Peterson, D. (1997, April). A great Chicago land grab. *Z Magazine.* Retrieved July 20, 2005, from http://www.zmag.org/ZMag/articles/apr97peterson.html

Piacente, M. (Executive Producer). (2004, April 1). *NBC5 News at Six* [Television broadcast]. Chicago: National Broadcasting Company.

Pratt, C. (1948). *I learn from children.* New York: Simon & Schuster.

Ravitch, D. (2000). *Left back: A century of failed school reform.* New York: Simon & Schuster.

Riley, D. W. (Ed.). (1993). *My soul looks back, 'less I forget: A collection of quotations by people of color.* New York: HarperCollins.

Schubert, W. H. (1989). On the practical value of practical inquiry for teachers and students. *Journal of Thought, 24*(1), 41–74.

Schubert, W. H. (1991). Teacher lore: A basis for understanding praxis. In C. Witherall & N. Noddings (Eds.), *Stories lives tell: Narrative and dialogue in education* (pp. 207–233). New York: Teachers College Press.

Schubert, W. H. (1992). Personal theorizing about teachers' personal theorizing. In E. W. Ross, J. W. Cornett, & G. McCutcheon (Eds.), *Teacher personal theorizing: Connecting curriculum, practice, theory, and research* (pp. 257–272). Albany: State University of New York Press.

Schubert, W. H. (1995). Students as action researchers: Historical precedent and contradiction. *Curriculum and Teaching, 10*(2), 3–14.

Schubert, W. H., & Lopez Schubert, A. L. (1981). Toward a curricula that are of, by, and therefore for students. *Journal of Curriculum Theorizing, 3*(1), 239–251.

Schwab, J. J. (1978). *Science, curriculum, and liberal education: Selected essays.* Chicago: University of Chicago Press.

Shute, A. (Executive Producer). (2004, March, 26). *ABC 7 News at Six* [Television broadcast]. Chicago: American Broadcasting Company.

Small Schools Workshop. (2007). *Small Schools Workshop info center.* Retrieved January 1, 2007, from http://www.smallschoolsworkshop.org/info1.html

Washington, B. T. (1901). *Up from slavery: An autobiography.* New York: Doubleday.

Weissman, D. (1996). Board replaces schools in neighborhoods with clout. *Catalyst Chicago.* Retrieved May 1, 2004, from http://www.catalyst-chicago.org/arch/11-96/116upd81.htm

Westheimer, J., & Kahne, J. (2004). What kind of citizen? The politics of educating for democracy. *American Educational Research Journal, 41*(2), 237–269.

Wood, G. H. (2005). *Time to learn. How to create high schools that serve all students* (2nd ed.). Portsmouth, NH: Heinemann.

Woodson, C. G. (1933). *The mis-education of the Negro.* Trenton, NJ: Africa World Press.

Zorn, E. (2004a, March 23). Students welcome all to see their dreary reality. *Chicago Tribune,* p. B1.

Zorn, E. (2004b, June 8). Despite school's closing, pupils' battle a success. *Chicago Tribune,* p. B1.

Index

About the Author

Brian D. Schultz is an assistant professor of education and honors faculty at Northeastern Illinois University (NEIU) in Chicago. He teaches courses in educational foundations, interpretive/critical research, contemporary issues in education, and curriculum. He has been recognized with the NEIU Faculty Excellence Award in Teaching. Prior to his role at NEIU, Brian taught in the Chicago Public Schools (CPS). In 2005, he received the Educator of the Year award from the Illinois Computing Educators for his teaching in CPS. Brian continues to work with and learn from many of his former students from the Cabrini Green neighborhood in which he taught.

Frequently traveling across the country, Brian speaks on democratic and progressive classroom ideals; theorizing with students; integrating curricula based on students' interests; problematizing race, class, and privilege; and curriculum as social action. Brian's work has appeared in scholarly publications such as *Curriculum Inquiry, Educational Studies, Equity & Excellence in Education, Journal of Educational Controversy, Schools,* and *The Handbook for Research on Teacher Education,* among others. In addition, he co-edited the volume *The Articulation of Curriculum and Pedagogy for a Just Society: Artistry, Advocacy, and Activism* (2007). He currently serves on the editorial boards of the *Journal of Curriculum & Pedagogy* and the *Journal of Educational Controversy,* chairs the American Educational Research Association's (AERA) Biographical & Documentary Research Special Interest Group (SIG), and is the recipient of the 2008 Early Career Award from both the AERA Critical Issues in Curriculum & Cultural Studies SIG and the Narrative & Research SIG.

Brian Schultz completed his undergraduate work in psychology and received a master's degree in experiential and elementary education at Miami University. He holds a Ph.D. in curriculum and instruction from the University of Illinois at Chicago. He and his wife, Jenn, live in Chicago with their daughter, Addison.